What is a Democrat?

Copyright 2024 by John Benedict
All rights reserved

Printed in the United States of America
No part of this book may be used or reproduced
in any manner whatsoever without written permission
except in the case of brief quotations
embodied in articles or reviews.

ISBN: 979-8-9916874-0-9

Published by
NRK Designs
Florida

What is a Democrat?

by
John Bendict

Table of Contents

1. Democracy and Socialism Defined

2. Democratic Convention of 2024

3. Kamala's Marketing Focus

4. Kamala Fact Checked

5. Illegal Immigration

6. Elections

7. Comparison to Trump

8. Experience of Kamala and Trump

9. Weaponizing the DOJ

10. Extreme Accusations

11. Major Campaign Lies

12. Kamala's Extreme Statements

13. Governor Walz

14. Walz Extols Kamala

15. Two Major Issues for Walz

16. Walz Gains Control of Minnesota

17. Abortion and Transgender Rules

18. Managing Tax Payer Money

19. Democratic Strategy

20. History of Democratic Presidents

21. Final Word

Prologue

How do you make sense of all the marketing, accusations and promises of a presidential campaign? And how do you define a Party that started with Andrew Jackson over 200 years ago. Certainly, there is a great deal of history to describe the direction, strategies, failures and accomplishments of the Democrats.

This is a brief but very current book to challenge the Democrats and bring much of the political conversation to a conclusion.

There seems to be a very successful effort to use the media bias, condemnation of Trump and general marketing propaganda to elevate Kamala Harris to an attractive nominee for president. Amazingly, she has had almost no interviews and no expressed specifics on what she would do as president. Instead, she cites optimistic slogans to define her qualifications and plans for the future. Her debate success was due strictly to her successful baiting of Donald Trump rather than an argument on what she would do as president with the problems of America, many of which were created or amplified under the Biden/Kamala administration the last 4 years.

One major concern is who will be president if Kamala is elected. Joe Biden has been senile for quite some time and reportedly has spent 40 % of his term on vacation which of course has not been covered by the media as Trump's occasional golf times have been. So that can only mean that some unelected board is running the country. Who is the board and with Kamala's lack of executive experience and accomplishments as VP would we also have an unelected board running the country if she should be elected?

This book is intended to question and identify the many holes in America and in the Democrat's approach to governance.

Chapter One
DEMOCRACY AND SOCIALISM DEFINED

First, we need to define the two classifications of government that will help define what democrats are promoting today.

Definition of Democracy:
A system of government in which the state's power is in the people or the general population of a state. Under a minimalist definition of democracy, rulers are elected through competitive elections while more expansive definitions link democracy to guarantees of civil liberties and human rights in addition to competitive elections.

Features of democracy oftentimes include freedom of association, personal property, freedom of religion and speech, citizenship, consent of the governed, voting rights, freedom from unwarranted governmental deprivation of the right to life and liberty, and minority rights.

Definition of Socialism:
Socialism was a revolutionary movement to capitalism that started in the mid to late 18th century. Karl Marx rode on this idea which was used to create the communism state, the USSR. Many properties are anti-capitalism concentrating on some form of social ownership for production, usually by the state. The state then determines the prices, markets and eliminates the profit element in commerce. They then provide the income to all citizens, not on what they earn

John Benedict

but as part of the state's formula of citizen participation

A variety of socialism is exercised with varying control from the state. If a state installs an education system, then rules are used to build different levels of participation. When health systems are provided by the state, that system is often called a socialistic action. Medicare could be called a socialistic action because the amount and rules are controlled by the state. Our education system could be called socialistic because it is governed by the state and the parents have little control.

Argentina is noted for the common method for converting from democracy to socialism. In order to receive votes politicians will often offer benefits from the state making citizens what appears to be a gift except the source of that gift are taxes of the citizens. The state, however governs the amount given, the taxes, and the rules of the benefit. When overdone as in the case of Argentina, it robs the citizens of motive, incentive and adds to the state the burden of managing the finances in a way that works. In the case of Argentina, the amount of gifts to the citizens was overdone and the management was insufficient for the gifts to balance so this resulted in a country without a healthy economy. In fact, stock brokers list Argentina as the last place to invest.

Chapter 2
DEMOCRATIC CONVENTION OF 2024

Before the Democratic convention, America made history by recognizing that we had been governed by an un known board since President Joe Biden had been suffering from senility for a considerable amount of time. Included in his vacancy of mind was his inattentive presence in his office. He vacationed 40% of the time during his presidency. The people responsible are the leaders of the Democratic Party who preferred power over American governance by an elected president enough to hide the problem from Americans. His public appearances may have been the major part of the 60% of activity that he had.

The office of president in the United States may be the most challenging office in the world. Domestic matters, foreign matters, America's unity, and major problems such as an exploding debt takes every minute of a president's time. With that enormous demand, he needs to be of sound mind, have great energy and presence in the office. The last thing we should have, is a secret ghost board running the country. Even now after Biden's senility has been displayed for all to see, he is still carrying the nuclear button. Is he doing that as a president or as a puppet.

The convention was an enthusiastic group of Democrats who went from grief when Biden's senility was recognized to the nomination of a much younger and attractive Kamala who has a big smile and great group attraction. Her experience and skill set were not a consideration.

Will we have that same unknown unelected board if Kamala is elected? With her lack of executive experience and her notable lack of accomplishment as the VP, one has to be concerned. If nothing else Kamala is unburdened by what has been.

The convention was filled with speeches, almost everyone criticizing and calling Trump names. Their whole speech content was crafted not to discuss the future but to remember cherished moments of being together: cheering from the bleachers on Friday night, call and response from pews on Sunday morning, watching Team USA win Olympic gold, and conversations with your best friend on girls' night out. the convention was a celebration, a coming out party so to speak in which there was new hope for their nominee to succeed against Donald Trump.

And they did it in short words and phrases Americans use every day. This was a change for Democrats. Out were abstract ideas, in were muscular verbs and concrete nouns. Out were 10-point policy speeches, in were stories of patriotism and service, sports and teamwork, family and faith.

The following words were the central themes of the convention. They are attractive words set in an unusual time when the last 3 and ½ years were governed by the nominee and the president who is stepping down. The failures are multiple and among the worst of any president in our history but these words below are placed as if we have not had freedom, joy and hope under their reign. But who cares. It feels so good:

Freedom: The abstract idea of "democracy" became the personal concrete noun "freedom." Americans weren't asked to save democracy. They were called to protect and regain their freedoms that democracy promised. Those freedoms affected "matters of home and heart" as Harris put it in her acceptance speech.

Joy: Joy is a word that you feel as you say it. House Democratic Leader Hakeem Jeffries (D-N.Y.) quoted Psalm 30:5 "...there will be joy in the morning." Kamala Harris with "her laugh and her light" was the source of that joy. Second Gentleman Doug Emhoff called her "a joyful warrior… She finds joy in pursing justice." Bill Clinton promised she would be the "president of joy." Joy is a magnet that draws volunteers into a collective effort, just as Harris's two grandnieces did as they taught the crowd (and America) how to say their auntie's name in a call and response of "comma-la."

Hope: "Hope is making a comeback," said Michelle Obama, echoing the winning theme of her husband's first campaign, setting him up to lead his speech with "I'm fired up" and the crowd roaring back "and ready to go." That 2008 rallying cry came not from him, but from a campaign worker in North Carolina—a reminder to talk like Americans if you want to inspire them.

Trump: "Throw as many negative comments about Trump as the many speakers can find, rather true, exaggerated or created. This must be included in every speech." By one count Trump was mentioned 271 times in the convention and of course not in a positive way. He was second only to Kamala.

Chapter 3
Kamala's Marketing Focus

Each Political Party has a marketing plan and no party has ever been more successful than the Democrats in finding votes. These are some of the items they use to accomplish that;

- Kamala stated that she would make sure everyone had a fair income. In her first campaign ad, she recast the Democratic agenda as centered on "freedom," saying the word four times to highlight her support for workers ("the freedom not just to get by, but get ahead"), gun safety laws ("the freedom to be safe from gun violence") and access to abortion ("the freedom to make decisions about your own body"). In case you somehow missed the message, the minute-long ad is set to Beyoncé's 2016 song "Freedom," which repeats the word another 10 times.

- "Our fight for the future is also a fight for freedom," she told the gathering of campaign staffers and volunteers. "Generations of Americans before us have led the fight for freedom from our founders to our framers, to the abolitionists and the suffragettes, to the freedom riders and farmworkers. And now I say team, the baton is in our hands."

- This message on freedom is a marketing statement but not a true statement. Freedom means having the ability to act on your own behalf without government dictation. Kamala represents the opposite. She is selling the idea that government will provide many services even some high level of income for all citizens. Of course, this income has to be paid and in a democracy that operates on freedom of work, the income is earned by work and effort. In a socialistic system, the income to insure everyone has a "fair" income is from tax money taking away the freedom from all taxpayers. This begins the hidden theme to take freedom from one person to give to another person by government over which the citizens have no control. This turns a democracy into a socialistic state. Newton's third law of motion is that for every action there is an equal and opposite reaction. Freedom is like that.

- Freedom from gun violence is another freedom that takes away the freedom for citizens to own guns. Granted we would like to have no gun violence but most murders are committed with un-registered guns and with more guns in America than citizens it would take an aggressive forceful act of government to take guns away from citizens as was done in Germany under Hitler and in the USSR by Stalin. Attempts have been made to pass gun laws to solve the problem but those gun laws have not been effective. In most cases, where the gun laws have been the strongest, the greatest gun violence occurs and often when the gun laws are the weakest, crime and gun violence is the least thanks in part to citizens providing their own protection. Criminals have sources for guns even if the law is anti-gun but the ordinary citizen does not have sources. Taking guns away from citizens who own guns for protection takes that protection away from citizens trying to protect themselves and making criminals who have no problem acquiring guns safer.

- Freedom to make decisions about your own body means that other bodies must die to give that freedom. Just as in the case of freedom of a "fair income" someone has to pay for that to happen. The reproductive "freedom" is only in the minds of those who believe that killing an unborn up to ½ hour before birth is legal while killing the unborn after birth is murder. Abortion also requires a mind that is only fixed on their pregnancy issue and the need for an emergency contraceptive instead of a human life that is taking shape inside her, that shape being able to live outside the womb in some cases. In the case of Minnesota even until birth. As a touch of realism, Harris would never get the chance to codify Roe v. Wade if elected because Congress "can never get this approved". So it doesn't matter what she says about going to Congress. The same is true of Republicans changing the abortion law in any way at a federal level.

- No system provides for complete freedom. Health is a good example. The ObamaCare version of America's health system has failed enormously and a socialistic approach may be the only way to correct it. At this point no one is in charge of pricing. Doctors, hospitals, labs, insurance, government and pharmaceutical all interact together meaning no one is in control of pricing. In fact, they act in a way that encourages price increases. We are now operating with enormous medical cost that doesn't even improve our longevity. We rank 26th in the world.

- Ironically our education system is socialistic and failing big time making our education system the 31st in the world and the most expensive. The socialistic system is dead and going downhill every year. All other countries have private education funded by government. Only a private system funded by the government will resolve this issue. Our socialistic system is run by education bureaucrats who are primarily concerned about continuing the present system and income for those working in the education system. A private system funded by the government is what all the leading education countries have. It is better and costs much less.

- I know it is ironic but I am claiming our socialist education system needs to be replaced by a private system while our private medical system needs to be replaced by a socialistic system but both systems have become so corrupted there is no practical way to correct them under their present form. The rest of the world does what I am proposing, a socialistic medical system and a private education system and they are vastly better than America's system.

- Inflation; "We are for those who have little wealth" says the Democrats. Yet inflation peeked twice during a Democratic White House. Jimmy Carter set a record and Joe Biden kept it up but the debt during Biden's time rose from 27 to 37 trillion with accompanying inflation. Debt rises when inflation is out of control. Inflation hurts people the most who are living from payday to payday. A typical family is now paying $900 per month more than under Trump in January of 2021. When groceries double in price it becomes very hard to pay the rent so inflation creates additional homeless among those who have little wealth. No presidency has hurt people living from paycheck to paycheck more than Biden's. The Democratic Party theme "we are for the little guy" should be changed to "the little guy will go homeless with governance by the Democrats".

- Calculating debt caused by both Trump and Biden is hard to analyze because of the pandemic. Both presidents threw too much money at the problem and both set pandemic rules that were very harmful to America. The question has not been answered which did the most damage – COVID or the rules set in place to defend against COVID. Both presidents were responsible for much of their debt but Trump's pandemic expenditures paid off in creating vaccines in record impossible time. Trump's tax bill was very bad timing because of the pandemic and losing the election to Biden. Biden continued throwing money at the pandemic and created additional costs and losses to family, education, business and work through the extreme rules characterized as necessary to combat the pandemic.

Biden cancelled much of Trump's plans which created an inflation spiral and prevented much of Trump's tax bill from fruition. Biden also set new rules making it more difficult to drill for oil. The result was a decrease in oil, dependence once again on foreign oil and 50-100% increase in fuel cost that affected all aspects of our life where transportation is involved. That created a great deal of inflation that compounded the problem and accelerated the debt. However, for both Biden and Trump, the last thing you do when the debt is soaring is increase spending and decrease income.

Of course, with higher spending and no commensurate increase for income, debt will have to be the source for the extra money spent. Already the interest on our national debt will soon exceed 1 trillion per year, just a little less than 25% of our tax income today. there is no plan and almost no discussion in the election rhetoric on this most important American problem. Incredibly the news focuses on migrants eating cats and a humorous statement about dictatorship.

Kamala is unburdened by what has been.

Chapter 4

Kamala Fact Checked

From FactCheck.org, the New York Times, and an article by Eugene Kiely also a fact checker.

1. Kamala repeats her statement that Trump will cut Social Security. Fact Check says Trump did not propose cutting Social Security's retirement benefits, and his budgets included bipartisan proposals to reduce the growth of Medicare without cutting benefits. "We will not cut one penny from Social Security and Medicare," Trump said in Grand Rapids, Michigan.
   In January 2023, when House Republicans were discussing ways to cut government spending, Trump said in a video: "Under no circumstances should Republicans vote to cut a single penny from Medicare or Social Security to help pay for Joe Biden's reckless spending spree."
   Clarification, July 25: We have updated this story to clarify that while Trump did not propose cuts to Social Security's retirement benefits as president, he did propose cutting the Social Security Disability Insurance and Supplemental Security Income programs.

2. Kamala accuses Trump of planning to use Project 2025 if elected. 2025 is a 900-page plan` written by some extreme conservatives mostly connected with Heritage Foundation. Trump says he has not read it. Trump described it at his Michigan rally as "seriously extreme." He added, "I don't know anything about it. I don't want to know anything about it."

    Project 2025 lays out "four goals and principles" for Medicare "reform," but there is nothing in the 900-plus page document that calls for cutting Social Security, which the authors of the project call a "myth."

3. Kamala says she will end America's housing shortage by tax breaks and $25,000 downpayment assistance for first time buyers and a $40 billion fund to help communities develop affordable housing. That might work but has potential problems such as someone taking a mortgage with the help of government but does not have enough income to sustain the mortgage as happened in the 2009 era causing a recession. Under Biden/Kamala housing costs have risen 30%. That is a major factor in housing shortage. Those with little wealth can't afford to live where they did. Many people are going homeless or downgrading to an apartment or trailer park.

4. Kamala wants to extend the Trump tax cut for individuals that expires in 2025 with changes to only those making less than $400,000 per year while increasing taxes for those above and on corporations. I don't have a problem with that unless the number of people that benefit is too great and adds significantly to our national debt and no doubt it will. I wrote my thoughts on corporate tax increases in another part of this paper. Corporations don't pay taxes. They just

mark it up and add to the cost of the product. The consumer pays the "tax" through the added price of the product. The other big negative is that we are less competitive overseas if we raise corporate taxes.

5. The removal of taxes on tips was Trump's idea and Kamala mimicked the idea. There is concern on how big that number could be causing the national debt to get larger. We know cutting taxes is a way to buy votes but America's future is to manage the debt and these programs will only increase the debt.

6. Kamala also claimed that Trump will enact a national sales tax and that has never been mentioned by Trump. Some thinks she might be saying that because of the tariffs Trump has said he will use to protect American workers. Trump added tariffs in his first term and accomplished more jobs in America and gained Mexico's agreement to manage border, etc. That was when Trump accomplished a large decrease in illegal immigrants. Biden/Harris has left almost all of the tariffs in place so that did not seem a problem until Kamala was campaigning.

7. Kamala claims Trump will be a dictator. Harris was referring to a comment that Trump made at a Fox News town hall in December. At the event, Sean Hannity gave Trump the chance to respond to critics who warned that Trump would be a dictator if elected to a second term. "Under no circumstances, you are promising America tonight, you would never abuse power as retribution against anybody," Hannity said. Trump responded, "Except for Day 1." And smiled.

   Trump went on to say, "We're closing the border. And we're drilling, drilling, drilling. After that, I'm not a dictator."

   Trump later claimed he was joking with

Hannity. In a Feb. 4 interview with Fox News' Maria Bartiromo, Trump said: "It was with Sean Hannity, and we were having fun, and I said, 'I'm going to be a dictator,' because he asked me, 'Are you really going to be a dictator?' I said, 'Absolutely, I'm going to be a dictator for one day.' Immediately I will cancel all of Biden's executive orders that didn't work and bring America back to a democracy.

8. Kamala says that Trump's personal life and the many indictments against him makes him unfit to govern. That is very argumentative since the indictments appear to be a weaponization by the Democrats to disqualify Trump. The indictments are unprecedented and far beyond any such actions with any other presidential candidate in America's history. Also, Kamala's personal life is kept quiet by the biased news media. Vice presidential nominee Kamala Harris had an extramarital affair with former San Francisco Mayor and California State Assembly Speaker Willie Brown, who gave her two political appointments that launched her political career. She was 29 and he was 60. The name for that relationship is probably not one that compliments a nominee for president.

It would be so refreshing if the democrats would discuss serious issues like the 21% increase in inflation that is decimating those of little wealth and the 15 to 20 million illegal immigrants that violated our immigration laws, causing numerous crimes, displacement of our workers, and adding $150.5 billion per year to our $36 trillion debt, instead of focusing on a remark by Trump or the old lie that Republicans are going to cut Social Security. That focus tells you a lot about what the Democrats have to offer.

9. In a July 18 speech in Fayetteville, North Carolina, Harris left the misleading impression that Trump was to blame for the loss of "tens of thousands" of manufacturing jobs. "So, Donald Trump tries to claim he brought back American manufacturing," Harris said. "The fact is, under Donald Trump, America lost tens of thousands of manufacturing jobs."

The fact is, those jobs were lost during the global COVID-19 pandemic. As of February 2020, the U.S. had added 414,000 manufacturing jobs under Trump, according the Bureau of Labor Statistics. But then the economic effects of the pandemic took hold. In the panic, the U.S. **lost 1.3 million manufacturing jobs** just in April of 2020.

Biden likes to brag about adding jobs but he takes as the low mark, a point in the pandemic when America was in really tough shape. The jobs added after the pandemic was a large number because there was a catch-up time and there were not enough people working or products available to fill the sudden need. Most of those jobs came back. The rest of Biden's term was a rush by supply to catch up with the lost COVID years and job growth was good. Since January 2021, the U.S. has added 762,000 manufacturing jobs but that is less than the single month lost in April 2020 due to COVID.

With the pandemic impacting jobs so much it is impossible to penalize or credit either presidents for jobs loss or gain.

Very interesting occurrence on jobs. Last week (August 22, 2024), the Labor Department reported that between early 2023 and early 2024 monthly job figures were overstated. The agency said the U.S. economy added 818,000 fewer jobs than previously stated, which was the biggest downward change since the financial crisis in 2009. What happened? Did Biden/Kamala lie about jobs anticipating the election?

Sen. Roger Marshall of Kansas and four other GOP senators want to know what in the Labor Department's reporting methodology "is malfunctioning so badly that it must revise its job numbers downward by almost a million jobs?"

A comparison of numbers by Biden/Harris to Trump/Pence is as follows according to factcheck.org.;

- Inflation under Trump was 7.6% and 19% for four years under Biden.
- Gasoline prices were $2.26 per gallon under Trump and 3.47 under Biden
- Crude oil production rose 27.9% under Trump and 15.3% under Biden
- Average weekly earnings rose 8.4% under Trump and fell 2.3% under Biden
- Home ownership rose 2.1% under Trump and fell .25% under Biden
- Trade deficit was up 36.3% under Trump and was up 22.3% under Biden. Trump brought the trade deficits down with tariffs and Biden kept the Trump tariffs.
- Consumer concerns dropped to 10% under Trump and rose to 30% with Biden

Employment cannot be compared because the pandemic created employment chaos. In one month during the critical April 2020 over a million jobs were lost. When the pandemic ended the lost jobs were recovered and additional jobs necessary to catch up with the latent demand.

Last week in North Carolina, Kamala Harris called for a new federal law to ban "price gouging on food." Such a law might be popular, but it would have, at best, no impact on grocery prices and might even make the problem worse. That's especially unfortunate because it detracts from all the federal policy changes that actually could reduce food prices. The evidence that price gouging was responsible for the post-pandemic spike in food prices is somewhere between thin and nonexistent. A recent report from the New York Federal Reserve found that retail food inflation was mainly driven by "much higher food commodity prices and large increases in wages for grocery store workers," while profits at grocers and food manufacturers "haven't been important."

Similarly, a 2023 report from the Kansas City Fed observed that rising food prices were overwhelmingly concentrated in processed foods, the prices of which are more sensitive to (and thus driven by) labor-market tightness and wage increases. Grocery profits did rise briefly during the pandemic, but the increase was the predictable result of increased demand (thanks to government stimulus along with more Americans eating at home) running headfirst into restricted supply (thanks to pandemic-related closures and supply-chain snarls, along with the war in Ukraine, a major food producer). In fact, expanding corporate profits frequently accompany bouts of heightened demand and inflation; the past few years have been no different.

Fortunately, Kamala is unburdened by what has been.

Chapter 5
Illegal Immigration

Kamala seldom mentions border security but in her convention speech she blamed the failure of the Biden/Kamala's border bill on the Republicans even though it was a last-minute attempt to minimize their failures in the illegal immigration world to save Democratic votes. Biden/Kamala, even though she was assigned the border management responsibility ignored all the illegal law-breaking immigrants arriving in this country by the millions during three plus years but realized now that the election is imminent and that the border invasion of illegals would cost them many votes had to find a way to blame the Republicans. The bill was very complicated and received negatives from both parties. For example, senator Cory Booker from New Jersey voted for it only because it included critical aid to Ukraine but otherwise, he publicly said he would not have voted for it because it was too restrictive. Not only the Democrat Booker had reservations about the bill but 5 other Democratic senators voted against the bill. The bill was not even acceptable to them.

    Why did the Biden/Kamala administration undo so many of the positive reforms enacted by the previous administration that worked better than any in decades? That is a big question. Why did Biden/Kamala change the rules to open up the border so wide to illegal immigrants. Is it to get more votes? They aren't eligible to vote but policing 15 million illegal immigrants in America when many of the polls are managed by Democrats is a possible advantage. 100,000 votes gave Biden the win last time. that is only one out of 1500.

What is a Democrat?

How big is the illegal immigrant problem? Yuma Mayor Douglas Nicholls told a Washington forum this week that the rise in illegal immigration is stressing health care and the nonprofits that help migrants in his town, and he's worried the situation will only get worse.

"Right now, our Border Patrol agents and our nonprofits are doing an amazing amount of work keeping Yuma safe," Nicholls said Wednesday, at a roundtable discussion on the border organized by Republican senators.

"As these (migrant) numbers continue to increase, it's going to be beyond their capability," he said. "From that perspective we have real concern about our health care system holding up, our nonprofit system holding up, and even our economy."

His comments come as apprehensions of immigrants at the southern border have surged to the highest level in decades, with more than 1.5 million arrests in the first 11 months of fiscal 2021.

But immigration advocates say those numbers can be misleading, since they may represent one migrant who is stopped multiple times at the border and turned away. They also argued that nonprofits were under stress by the pandemic before immigration numbers started rising in the last year of the Trump administration.

Apprehensions measure events, not individuals, said Jessica Bolter, associate policy analyst at the Migration Policy Institute, which is why "we can't use apprehension numbers to represent the total number of unique different migrants coming to the border."

Bolter said that "repeat crossing rates have skyrocketed in 2021," and that Border Patrol agents do not arrest every migrant trying to get through. Because of that, she said it does not "necessarily mean that the number of individuals caught at the border was the highest on record, and it also does not mean that the number of individuals released into the U.S. was the highest on record."

Whether it is the highest on record or not, speakers at Wednesday's event laid the blame for the "unprecedented surge in illegal crossings at our southern border" at the feet of President Joe Biden.

Residents that live on the border state that "Everything is literally open. People just come across, wait to get picked up and get sent along somewhere in the U.S," said the Yuma resident. One sponsor received 1800 illegal migrants, an absurd number considering that they are met to be family.

Harris has often been described as the "border czar" for her role in immigration assigned to her by President Biden, although some media outlets sought to dispute the title and argued it's unfair to assign her blame for security problems.

A Del Rio, Texas gun shop owner called out the vice president for doing "nothing" for border security and said Kamala has never been to the border, although in 2021, Harris visited a processing center in El Paso. The Del Rio resident also gave Harris a zero for her handling of immigration and said the border crisis will just "get worse" under a Harris administration.

The open borders are a serious crime and cost problem for Texas so Texas began to patrol the border as an adjunct to the federal government, whose border control was not even close to being sufficient and would you believe the White House has used the justice system to try to stop them from protecting themselves.

Migrant crossings at the southern border, which had been increasing in the last months of the Trump administration, skyrocketed after Biden entered office because Biden removed many of the actions that Trump initiated to protect America and honor the law. Biden also rolled back a number of Trump-era initiatives and attempted to place a moratorium on deportations. With numbers rising quickly, Biden told reporters that Harris would be put in charge of tackling "root causes" – issues like climate change, poverty and violence the administration believes was driving migrants north.

"There's about five other major things she's handling, but I've asked her, the VP, today — because she's the most qualified person to do it — to lead our efforts with Mexico and the Northern Triangle and the countries that help — are going to need help in stemming the movement of so many folks, stemming the migration to our southern border," he said. How wrong could a president be?

What is a Democrat?

It quickly led to Harris being dubbed by media outlets and Republicans as the "border czar". The White House rejected that title, but it has stuck with her ever since and made her a figurehead along with DHS Secretary Alejandro Mayorkas for the crisis. As a border czar, the first thing a competent manager would do is connect with the DHS secretary to define the problem and organize a plan.

While Texas has been reliably red in presidential elections since 1980, Arizona has become a significant swing state. In 2020, Joe Biden narrowly carried it to become the first Democrat to win the state since Bill Clinton in 1996. It is expected to be hotly contested again in 2024; no Republican has ever won the White House without also winning the state.

With illegal immigration now costing *$150.7 billion annually (for 4 years that would be $.6 trillion)*, the burden inevitably trickles down to the taxpayer. Individually, the FAIR study found that each illegal alien or their U.S.-born child costs the U.S. $8,776 annually. Estimates of the number of illegals since Biden became president is 15 to 20 million. The population of New York City is only 9 million. The $150.7 billion cost does not include the cost to states, counties and cities who have to assimilate and care for these millions of illegal immigrants.

Biden/Harris in mid-2024 claimed a major decrease in illegal immigrants but some report that they have begun a large system of flying illegals into all parts of America without going through the border process. The number have not changed just the paper process. Biden/Kamala are using the same process that they used to cut the crowd on the United States side of the border by flying immigrants to all parts of the country, which they have done for years.

Adam Shaw reported the above from Arizona, Nikolas Lanum and Elizabeth Heckman reported from Texas.

Chapter 6
Elections

President Biden would veto a House Republicans Budget Bill requiring proof of citizenship to vote in federal elections the White House announced.

Election rules; In a statement of administration policy, the White House said the GOP proposal would needlessly set government spending "at insufficiently low levels" for six months, rather than providing a short-term stopgap to give Congress more time to pass new spending bills. Continuing resolutions, or CRs, the congressional parlance for stopgaps extending current funding and policies into the next fiscal year, should always be as short as possible, the White House said a six-month stopgap is "especially irresponsible" in holding defense funding and policies stagnant because it "would erode our military advantage relative to the People's Republic of China, degrade readiness, and fail to provide the support our troops deserve," the administration said.

The March 28 end date of the stopgap also comes "dangerously close to the deadline when across-the-board cuts would come into place next year, as dictated by the Fiscal Responsibility Act of 2023," the statement said. The White House slammed House Republicans' inclusion of "unrelated cynical legislation that would do nothing to safeguard our elections, but would make it much harder for all eligible Americans to register to vote and increase the risk that eligible voters are purged from voter rolls." The proof of citizenship requirement is "unnecessary" because it is already illegal for

What is a Democrat?

noncitizens to vote in federal elections, the administration said, adding that "states already have effective safeguards in place to verify voters" eligibility and maintain the accuracy of voter rolls," as the bill seeks to mandate at the federal level.

Of course, these arguments are transparent. There are reports of illegal migrants signing up to vote with no policing by the Democrats, just encouragement. There are millions of people on the voting rolls that have moved or are dead opening up a wide door for fraud. The blue states also fight to the death to eliminate the need for an ID. Without an ID and with millions of names of people who have died or moved on the rolls, there is a vast opening for fraud. The only possible reason for insisting that voting is better monitored is to allow fraud to be easier.

The media and Democrats claim there is no fraud. Papers cite people caught in fraud every year and it is in all the papers – liberal and conservatives. What we don't know is how many because the voting is suppose to be seen only by the voter and a counting machine. Also states such as Minnesota fight constantly to protect the voting system that they have created so that it is very difficult to police. Minnesota's Democratic Secretary of State has had years of court battles including at the Minnesota Supreme Court all in an effort to thwart the efforts of Judicial Watch and Common Cause.

Other instances that are public knowledge:
- Norm Coleman was the current Senator who was challenged by Al Franken in the election of 2009. Al franken lost the election by over 500 votes so a recount was ordered. He still lost the vote so they recounted again. This time he won by a few hundred. In one case a precinct worker claimed he forgot some ballots in his trunk so weeks after the election he was allowed to submit them.
- A former Texas voting official seeking "peace of mind" says he certified enough fictitious ballots to steal an election 29 years ago and launch Lyndon B. Johnson on a path that led to the presidency.

- The 1960 presidential election was the closest of the twentieth century when measured by the popular vote. John F Kennedy managed narrow margins in a number of critical states to carry him to victory over Richard M. Nixon. Because of the close call in Illinois (Kennedy won by an official count of 8,858 votes), the unsavory reputation of the Chicago Democratic organization, and certain newspaper reports, Republicans and Nixon became convinced that they had been cheated out of enough votes to have swung the state into the Republican column. This article analyzes these Republican allegations, which have been widely accepted, on the basis of two partial recounts of paper ballot precincts which were conducted in Cook County (Chicago) in the aftermath of the 1960 elections. This analysis shows that there was a pattern of miscounting votes which worked to the advantage of all Democratic candidates involved in the recount. The analysis also shows, however, that of the Republican candidates deprived of votes, Richard M. Nixon suffered the least. By comparing the two recounts and by making estimates based upon them it is possible to approximate a minimum number of votes Nixon lost as the result of election irregularities in Chicago. This figure of slightly less than 8,000 votes is not sufficient to make a convincing case that Nixon was cheated out of Illinois' electoral votes.

No doubt there have been thousands of elections where the winner benefitted from fraudulent votes and mishandling of ballots. When the media acts as if this never happens, they show an extreme bias.

Chapter 7
KAMALA and TRUMP compared

Vice President Kamala Harris in 2019 supported a suite of left-wing causes as follows:

- Cuts to the Immigration and Customs Enforcement operations and taxpayer-funded transition surgeries.
- Support for decriminalization of all drug possession, according to the ACLU questionnaire. That would include fentanyl.
- End the unfair incarceration of thousands of individuals, families and children, so you let them be free to go where they want in America.
- A decrease in funding to ICE. Today ICE cannot begin to keep up with the job. Too few people and too few tools.
- Rein in ICE detainers on illegal immigrants who encounter state and local law enforcement.
- Gangs are showing up in many of our cities from the illegal immigration. For example, police have identified what they say are 10 members of a notorious Venezuelan gang threatening residents of a Colorado town, with some crimes dating back to late last year. The Tren de Aragua (TdA) members have been known to Aurora Police Department for several months, but

- the town entered the national spotlight after a video showing violence in an apartment building went viral. Aurora PD said Wednesday that TdA members had been "committing acts of violence against members of the migrant community" in the town.
- By contrast, Mr. Trump has pushed for border walls and pledged a massive deportation program if he wins in November.
- On transgender issues, Ms. Harris said she would support transition surgeries for persons in prisons.
- "It is important that transgender individuals who rely on the state for care receive the treatment they need, which includes access to treatment associated with gender transition,"
- Mr. Trump, by contrast, frequently criticizes Ms. Harris running mate, Minnesota Gov. Tim Walz, for his policy support for transgender issues. Allowing children to decide to make a sexual change that might not be reversible is an extraordinary step. Children are often not mature enough to recognize such a deep significant problem. Bear in mind that children are often swayed by their peers by fads and the current popular idea that will change from generation to generation. Children need to mature into their 20's to make major health decisions such as sex change.
- Ms. Harris said she moderated her views while working beside President Biden but she insisted her "values have not changed." That is a very contrary idea, to change her ideas but not her values when the idea change is a value change.
- Kamala is campaigning in a way seldom if ever done before. She is talking change to correct all the problems that America has when the problems that

What is a Democrat?

America has are those in large part created by her and Joe Biden's last 4 years of their administration. Normally one talks about the problems created by the opposition not problems created by oneself' s.

- Kamala is also very active in negative attacks against Trump that have no impact on managing America. Some examples are Trump's comedic remark about being a dictator and the 2025 agenda written by Heritage Foundation and not even read by Trump. To blow that up to a serious discussion especially after proving that is not his intent in his 4 years of being the President is a reach beyond absurd. The ill-advised comment about migrants eating pets fall in that same category. Kamala makes those types of comments but no comments about specific things she intends to do. Her comments about what she will do as president are all very general in nature with no specifics.

- Kamala's primary action against inflation seems to be the blocking of grocery prices, an act that has been proven harmful throughout the world many times. Inflation was not a problem under Trump but actions by Biden/Kamala set off one of the largest inflationary spirals in American history. Trump's normal inflation rate of 2.5% per year was quickly followed by Biden's 9% in the first year.

- Under Trump the economy was of almost no concern to Americans. Under Biden/Kamala it is one of if not the top concern.

- Other changes; Under Trump, we had drilled for more oil than we used and Biden/Kamala stopped that. The border was in the best control for decades and now we have an invasion greater than ever in our history creating massive problems. The economy was doing great and now is the top concern of voters. There were no wars and Trump had essentially stopped the war in Afghanistan and the Taliban had agreed to our evacuation plan. Biden/Kamala's evacuation from Afghan was the biggest debacle in American history. Biden/Kamala basically turned the evacuation of the US over to the Taliban. The height of COVID had occurred with Trump achieving vaccine in record time. Biden/Kamala created additional rules that stopped our economy, robbed small business, and served only as a big profit for pharmaceuticals. The biggest problem was our massive debt to which the Biden/Kamala administration had contributed a great deal. She seems to have ignored that massive problem. Instead, she focuses on personal issues of Trump's which are in large part created by the Democratic Party and does not have an impact on America. She also tries to make a big problem over a wrong interpretation of something he says. This has to be the most disingenuous and hypocritical campaign ever run.

Vice President Kamala Harris will push to increase the corporate tax rate to 28% from the current 21% her campaign said Monday, the first day of the Democratic National Convention in Chicago. The corporate tax reduction by Trump was done to be competitive in the world. We were at 35%. Ireland was at 15% and others were in the 20% range. At 28% we will reduce our competitiveness internationally and the extra taxes will be added to the cost of the product. The tax will only be passed on to the consumer so the increased corporate tax is a tax on buyers. What corporations will cut their profit to pay a tax? No business man does that, especially when they know all of their competition will have to do the same. This common cry to tax corporations displays ignorance about finances and business and something only a socialist would say.

Coming days after she unveiled a four-part economic package that would provide tax relief to working and middle-class Americans, the corporate tax proposal marks Harris' first effort to detail how she would pay for her policy platform should she win the presidential election. The tax relief that she preaches is actually the retainage of the tax cut that Trump passed. Tax relief is a myth. Trump preaches the same thing. We went from a deficit of $10 trillion after Bush to $36 trillion today and we are budgeting a deficit each year of $1.5 to 2 trillion dollars each year. We can only survive by increasing taxes and cutting spending. Buying votes with debt is a terribly unwise and destructive idea for America.

- "As President, Kamala Harris will focus on creating an opportunity economy for the middle class that advances their economic security, stability, and dignity," campaign spokesperson James Singer said in a statement. "Her plan is a fiscally responsible way to put money back in the pockets of working people and ensure billionaires and big corporations to pay their fair share." And we will make snow in July!!! What an absolutely inane statement. Creating economy can only be done by the government providing money, tax relief or benefits. That means a larger mortgage on Americans. It is not a gift but simply adding to the mortgage when the government already has a debt of 36 trillion?? Kamala is not the only one making stupid statements. Trump also is talking about another tax break. Heaven help us if no one sees that we are in a debt hole we cannot extricate ourselves from and must not dig deeper.

- In regard to billionaires paying more taxes, our extremely complicated tax rules were designed by both Democrats and Republicans. It provides many opportunities for those who can afford the tax lawyers to reduce their taxes. It is a mega-mistake by congress but I see no one who will stand up and rewrite the rules. Realize even with these rules, the top 10% of taxpayers pay more tax than the bottom 90%. So, the rich do pay taxes but the statement suggests that the bottom 90% don't pay enough taxes. If the bottom 10% paid 40% of the taxes, would we have a debt problem? The bottom 90% should be paying more taxes too but tax should not be exclusive to them. Everyone has to be financially responsible. We cannot afford to make the government account for the inability of people to provide for themselves. That is giving free lunches to everyone and the government has no money to use for that purpose.

- The rate hike, which is in line with what President Joe Biden has supported but less than the 35% rate that Harris proposed during her 2020 presidential campaign, would reverse a major component of former President Donald Trump's 2017 Tax Cuts and Jobs Act. That law reduced the corporate income tax rate from 35% – and it doesn't expire, unlike the TCJA's individual income tax provisions, which lapse after 2025.

- Raising the corporate tax rate would reduce the deficit by $1 trillion over the next decade, according to the Committee for a Responsible Federal Budget. The watchdog group estimates the price tag of Harris' economic package would be $1.7 trillion over the next decade. That does not include the increase in product cost that would accompany the increased

corporate taxation. If you included the increased product cost, raising the corporate tax rate would actually be a negative to our debt.
- Trump, on the other hand, has said he would cut taxes on businesses, as well as provide relief for Americans. Trump would like to lower the corporate tax rate to as low as 15% – though he acknowledged in an interview last month with Bloomberg Businessweek that reducing it that much would be hard. Trump doesn't get it either. We are in debt trouble and the last thing we need is less tax income.
- Why did Kamala support a ban on fracking? Is her change of heart, which she says is no change, due just to the election. What happens after the election?
- Is governor Walz's law to abort a baby up to the very moment of birth her desire as well?
- Will you keep the laws and subsidies to drive electric cars?
- We know Kamala will be unburdened by what has been.

Chapter 8
Experience of Kamala and Trump

Experience —
- Trump had decades of experience as a CEO. Managing many major issues at one time is common for him. When he went into the White House, he said it was foreign and many of his appointments were Washington veterans providing Washington advice. It took him a number of years to correct that and build an effective team working for America instead of Washington. His next term would provide the greatest combination of experience and knowledge ever in the White House. He knows now exactly what to do and how to do it. For example, he used the tariff threat on Mexico to resolve the issues of Mexico feeding off United States and included in the agreement was Mexico helping to close down the border and it made a major difference. I look forward to him recovering that border advantage that Biden lost and using the tariff threat or money against China, who has been eating our lunch.

- Trump fell into the foreign affairs management quite naturally. He announced to Russia and everyone else watching that he was dangerous when he attacked

What is a Democrat?

a Russian airport in Syria for chemically bombing Syrian civilians. He wiped out ISIS in months. Obama had been playing with that card for years with no appreciable success. He coerced NATO nations into sharing more of the cost. He settled North Korea down. He sanctioned Iran and almost broke them financially until Biden came along and saved them enabling them to support the many terrorists in the Middle East. Trump also scared the Taliban by showing the leader the picture of his home and telling him what would happen to it if he didn't stop. They had an "understanding" so Trump organized an evacuation and then lost the election. Biden gave up the best tool we had, our air base and created the worst debacle of America's history. Has anyone ever turned their evacuation over to their enemies, who happen to be terrorists? No one could be that dumb. Oh, but someone was.

- Kamala on the other hand has had no CEO experience to my knowledge. She held a high position in California that was primarily a technical leadership. She was a senator but only one of 100. She is attractive and had a big smile but her speeches are just slogans, cheerleading and very general stuff. The only specific idea is to freeze taxes on groceries. All the papers say that is a bad idea and that many countries (and even Nixon) tried to freeze prices and that freeze had the reverse effect.

    Like Biden, Kamala, being unable to be the CEO of America will have to just be the visible part of the presidency. All the leadership and specifics will be done by others. There is already a strategy to not expose her to tough questions or technical speeches. She is great at the cheerleading with a big smile and blasting her opponent with made up 5th grade stuff like the dictator remark but not visibly competent in technical matters on her feet, just like Biden who has never been quick or competent without a script even before his senility.

Kamala is clearly unburdened by what has been.

Chapter 9
WEAPONIZING DEPARTMENT OF JUSTICE

Political attacks on the opposition includes the many indictments filed against Trump the election year. This is clearly political weaponizing of the DOJ. Jack Smith was the point man for the Democrats in his DOJ attack on Trump but he was stripped of his special counsel title by a federal judge in Florida, and he lost 6-3 in the Supreme Court on the critical issue of presidential immunity. Despite the setbacks, he just took another shot at former President Donald Trump in the hopes of bringing him down before the November election. Many likely assumed the case was dead, considering the legal drubbing Mr. Smith just received. But this determined prosecutor moved back to the United States from The Hague for the once-in-a-lifetime opportunity of sending a Republican candidate to jail. He's not going back now.

Bragg, the attorney for NYC campaigned on the basis that he would indict Trump. Bragg was also supported in a large way by Soros who has an international goal of changing democracy through Soros PAC. Bragg chose an indictment that would not have been used with any other American citizen. He has focused on a case with many holes in it, something a competent attorney would not do. Contrary to the Trump approach, Bragg has let violent criminals go resulting in crime once again being common and overwhelming in NYC. An example is a violent criminal with nearly 90 arrests, that has been in state prison twice was arrested for a felony robbery. Bragg's office reduced the felony to a misdemeanor and released him. this means that a crime that makes the citizens of NYC unsafe is let free while Bragg spends an enormous amount of taxpayer money to indict a former president of a crime that has multiple holes in it and would not have been pursued by a competent attorney.

The Department of Justice, the same one that Jack Smith represents, cautions prosecutors against filing cases involving political candidates in the 60 days before an election. Ballots start hitting mailboxes in several states in early September, and in-person voting begins on Sept. 20 in Virginia. The 2024 election is already underway.

According to DOJ's Justice Manual, "Federal prosecutors and agents may never select the timing of any action, including investigative steps, criminal charges, or statements, for the purpose of affecting any election."

Mr. Smith's actions seem carefully timed. As soon as Mr. Smith had the opportunity, he ran to a grand jury of Democrats in the District to obtain this new indictment against Mr. Trump, which he presented on Tuesday to Judge Tanya Chutkan. Considering Judge Chutkan's lack of sympathy for Mr. Trump (she was appointed by then-President Barack Obama), the court will likely overlook the rushed indictment's deficiencies and assist Mr. Smith in reaching his Nov. 5 target.

Chapter 10
Extreme Accusations

Trump has had two assassination attempts in 2024. The culprits are apparently men who have extreme agendas or are mentally unhealthy. However, it would be interesting to discuss what caused them to chose Trump and not Biden or Harris. It very well could be the continuous attacks of Trump for 8 years by the media and the Democrats. The attacks have been daily and without the need for cause. When the first assassination failed a considerable number of Democrats were sorry it missed. That was actually shown on You Tube to just mention one source

Walz accused the Republicans of burning books because they don't want some books in the library. Apparently Walz would like to have children of any age have access to books with pornography, how to make a bomb etc. in the library. His inference is that he wants all books to go into the library. If that is his version of free speech why not put those things on TV too? They tried to tie Vance to disrespecting the service when he criticized Walz for lying about his military record. Two totally disconnected issues.

Then there is the made-up stuff such as Trump will destroy Social Security and Medicare. He will add a national sales tax. He will start a war etc.

Instead of arguing about a $36 trillion debt, 15 million illegal immigrants, 19% inflation that is continuing, a health care system that is overpriced, an education system that is 31rst in the world, and the enormous debt, the Democrats would show more concern by discussing solutions to those enormous problems.

I could continue with America's problems such as under servicing our people, a million abortions each year, crime rampant in our cities, drugs killing a couple hundred people every year (in Biden's 4 years we lost almost double the people that we lost in WWII). The Democrats are inventing issues that are not even real. Is this election about America or about power?

Chapter 11
Major Campaign Lies

The Democrats claim that Trump will do outrageous things in the next four years. Why would he not have done them in his first four? Obviously, they are meant to distract you from the fact that life was many times better when Trump was in the White House. Inflation was below 8% for all 4 years, oil and gas were plentiful and low in price, none of our enemies or potential enemies wanted to mess with Trump, the border was more secure than it had been for decades, protests were not filling the airwaves, the police were not being disrespected, crime was not rampant, housing had modest gains, Trump was ending the war in Afghan, etc. So, it is only smart to go on offense with absurd lies that the liberal faithful will believe and some of the other uninformed voters. Here is a list of some of the offensive offense.

Republicans will gut social security and Medicare (a very popular democratic lie). For example, Jeb bush was running even with the Democrat for Florida's governor race a few decades ago. The day before election all the people in the elderly category were called and told that Jeb would eliminate social security. As farfetched as that is, enough seniors believed it to give the Democrat a very narrow win. The Democrat who won because of this lie even confessed to the lie some years later. Trump had a chance to do what the Dems accuse him of planning to do but he was president for 4 years and never did anything close to the Democrats accusations. He has said repeatedly that he would not touch a dime of social security or

Medicare but since the Democratic lie works for so many voters (most of all who are ignorant) the Dems profit from the lie;

Republicans will ban abortion across America with or without congress (that may be about as farfetched as you can get. Abortion was just given back to the states and most of the states legalized it. Walz wants everyone to kill their unborn babies. He doesn't want anyone to save their unborn babies if they want to save them but are in an uncomfortable position with their pregnancy); Even though a vast number of voters don't want abortion, Walz doesn't want them to have it, even if they vote for their state to be anti-abortion. Just saw Senator Elizabeth Warren interviewed on the election and her whole speech was selling the ideas that if Trump was elected, they would make abortion illegal in the whole country. How does any politician have the audacity to speak such obvious lies?

Sarafina Chitika, a spokesperson for the Kamala Harris-Tim Walz ticket for the White House, accused Donald Trump of allowing Louisiana women to bleed to death because of his fights involving Roe v. Wade. This is not simple politicking. Democrats have become so brazenly open with their ugly, lying language that they're actually making the devil envious. It's like that old saying, hell hath no fury like a leftist lady kept from her tax-paid abortion.

The unfortunate fact is that many believe that ridiculous statement. "How Kamala Harris targeted pro-life pregnancy centers in California," Catholic News Agency reported just a few days ago. In other words, she didn't just support a woman's right to abort — she took it a step further and actively attacked those who offered options to abortion. That's evil. That's evil personified. That's today's Democrat Party.

Trump will become a dictator if he is elected. Another farfetched highlight by the Party that has nothing to brag about for the last four years except COVID, inflation, Debt, more gangs, 15 million more illegal immigrants some of whom are criminals, terrorists, prisoners, mental patients and many with no work skills.

That the Republicans will only serve the rich people and extreme voices in our country and that Democrats are for the people with no wealth. Under Trump we had the best economy in years and the biggest beneficiaries were the people living on a small income and the middle class. Under Biden/Kamala, people are struggling greatly. Income has actually gone down 2.4%.

Contrary to the rhetoric, the Democrats are the wealthy Party. The Democrat's coffers for the campaign are full. The Democrats have a tremendous advantage in campaign money because so many billionaires and rich people are Democrats. The decades old lie of Democrats that the Republicans are all rich and favor the rich has expired. The richest people in this country and in congress are Democrats.

She is clearly unburdened by what has been.

Chapter 12
Kamala's Extreme Comments

Candidates change position as election time draws near. Note In her interview with Dana Bash, according to a clip released Thursday afternoon by CNN, Ms. Harris said that those reversals don't mean her values are different. However;

During her failed 2020 presidential bid, Ms. Harris advocated for a national ban on fracking, the decriminalization of illegal border crossings and the elimination of private health insurance. Now she does not take those positions.

"In her interview with Dana Bash, according to a clip released Thursday afternoon by CNN, Ms. Harris said that those reversals don't mean her values are different.

"My values have not changed. So that is the reality of it. And four years of being vice president, I'll tell you, one of the aspects, to your point, is traveling the country extensively," she said. How absurd is it to campaign on change when the last four years that you want to change are your own work?

Kamala was adamantly against fracking for natural gas in 2019 and never reversed her position until this election. Now in western Pennsylvania, the bright spot for fracking she supports fracking realizing she will lose Pennsylvania if she doesn't change her mind. Ending fracking will end a very big industry in Pennsylvania. In fact, she was adamantly and emphatically against fracking when she ran for president early in the 2020 Democratic primary cycle (she bowed out in December 2019), and she was an original co-sponsor of the

What is a Democrat?

Green New Deal, which sets its sights on eliminating fossil-fuel use.

She'll never sound credible on the fuel subject. She only says what she has to say to fool voters.

In that vein, she's been a major cheerleader for the Biden-Harris efforts to increase our debt to pay Americans to buy electric vehicles that they clearly do not want, regardless of how much her campaign says she doesn't want to require that anymore.

She stole former President Donald Trump's proposal to stop taxing tips for service industry workers and somehow discovered a child tax credit proposal even though she voted against it as a senator when it was part of the Trump tax cut package in 2017.

This is clearly an idea to buy votes.

Placed in charge of the Biden-Harris administration's alleged strategy to address illegal immigration, she has overseen the open border of the last 4 years. Now, she is masquerading as an immigration hawk. Her television ads even have images of Mr. Trump's border wall, a national security measure that she once called "un-American." She has been quite clear in her views on illegal border crossing and has said multiple times that she does not believe it should be a crime. Today, of course, that tune has changed.

She has consistently supported the "defund the police" movement but is now desperately trying to walk that back as it has had a deadly impact on crime.

The list goes on, one item after another, and she repudiates herself over and over. During the debate the interviewer's fact checked Trump repeatedly but not once did they fact check Kamala. She needed to be fact checked on her accusation regarding 2025, immigration claims, Afghan answers, inflation answers, accusation that Trump will nationalize no abortion, that Trump lies and she doesn't, accusing Trump of adding tariffs when Biden/Kamala kept the tariffs that Trump instituted, fact checked on her statement that she knows the border laws are broken but doesn't acknowledge this was done under Biden/Harris.

Debate Sept. 10. The debate was not very informative unless you are a political guru and know all the issues and the position each candidate has. Then you could have an idea what was false and what was fact. Kamala took questions and ignored answering them instead saying something about being raised in a single parent family and how hard her mother worked. Then she would veer off and bait Trump by saying he lied about something or make some very severe accusations such as Trump, if elected would make abortion illegal in the whole country;

Kamala stated somethings she will do if elected but they are all very general and are clearly an advertisement instead of a plan. For example, she will help people buy houses but she does not say what the source will be for the money. Kamala also spent a great deal of time on her number 1 item, abortion. She proudly claimed it was all for women's health and she attacked Trump by saying he would outlaw abortion if he was elected.

She is clearly unburdened by what has been.

Chapter 13
Governor Walz

Walz is a great study of the Democratic Party. I lived in Minnesota for decades so this is a detailed look at the governor starting with his convention speech which revealed his extreme excitement at the possibility of being elected VP. He started with all the endearing stuff about growing up in a small town and rising through a great life from teacher to coach to congressman to governor to now a nominee. That is an exceptional experience.

A local private school superintendent believes Gov. Tim Walz's policies have had a "negative impact" on education in Minnesota, suggesting he "broke trust" with residents during the coronavirus pandemic. A former student said about Walz as his teacher "He yelled at students constantly. He would treat conservative students poorly and he would one side his teaching. If you were liberal, he liked you, and if you were conservative, he treated you like garbage. He was not a kind person.

He does not qualify as a traitor but his boasting during the campaign of taking a weapon in to war was a pure fabrication and nothing but an effort to use his service time to the maximum advantage.

Gov. Walz on taking office in 2019, was limited by a one-seat Republican majority in the state Senate. COVID hit in the spring of 2020. He declared a state of emergency on March 25, 2020 and ruled by decree for 15 months.

A former governor, Arne Carlson voted for Walz in the first

election because he felt Walz was impartial for a democrat. Arne having been a former governor was used in the beginning for questions but as Walz became more powerful he became more liberal and Arne soon regretted voting for him. One big issue for Arne is spending $800 million for two new buildings that were not needed. Those buildings now house not only staff for the legislature but 300 partisan staffers hired and managed by party caucuses but paid by the public coffers. Arne described this group as a fulltime mini-congress with large partisan armies dedicated to social interests and incumbent protection rather than voluntary service. Walz has set up his own little kingdom.

In November 2022 Mr. Walz was elected to a second term, and the DFL won majorities in both chambers of the Legislature. In the preceding two years the state had accumulated an $18 billion budget surplus. Taxpayers expected a refund but with the DFL in full control, Mr. Walz and the Legislature only returned $1 billion and added the rest to their budget so that they could institute the greatest amount of spending ever on infrastructure, education and other programs that will burden the state for years. Even with all that extra money they have also raised taxes. The education money keeps growing but the results keep falling. Thanks to the pandemic restrictions dictated by governor Walz, the basic education such as reading has dropped 25%.

He said he learned in congress to work across the aisle but as governor the last two years he defeated the other side on every measure because with majorities in the House and Senate he had no limitations and his true political beliefs surfaced. He is a strong socialist and rejects some of the basic principles of Christianity, some of whose principals are believed by other religions like Muslims.

His socialism was explained when he showed pride in furnishing 2 meals a day for students K-12. He believes that is wonderful but doesn't mention how it is paid. First of all, the people who pay are all tax payers. They are paying for two meals for students who have parents almost all of who can afford two meals a day. Imagine how many millionaires are having taxpayers pick up the check for their kids.

Secondly, the fraud that happened in this program is several times greater than the food budget associated with the pandemic. His carelessness in being a good steward was not only demonstrated here but seems to be a habit with the governor because he had the two major fraud problems, food fraud for his two meals a day at school and the pandemic help. they were similar in size. Minnesota had the most fraud of any state on the pandemic. Just those two frauds amounted to over $600 million.

His socialism exploded with a 20% increase in Minnesota expenditures in one year, keeping an $18 billion surplus from the previous year to spend in 2024/2025 and raising taxes in many areas. That is what socialism does. It gives a lot away to get power but it requires more taxes, enough for the give aways and the government overhead to handle the giveaways. Fraud seems to be a consistent problem especially in Minnesota. The more money the Government gives away the more fraud and corruption. Minnesota Is a high-priced state, costing 2 1/2 times more than a conservative state like Florida per person.

Walz included the usual lies about Republicans. According to Walz Republicans will jack up costs on middle-class families (after Biden/Kamala increased cost during their term of 21%); repeal the affordable Care Act (Republicans tried once and failed and now America's medical cost per person is 50% greater than the second most expensive country in the world and the results of spending all of this money has no reward. Americans have a longevity of only 26st in the world). With or without ObamaCare, America's health system is among the worst in the world;

Chapter 14
Walz Extols Kamala

Walz tells us;

1. That Kamala has fought on the side of the American people taking on predators and fraudsters (in the pandemic fiasco under Biden/Kamala, nearly $500 billion was fraudulently stolen from the pandemic money mostly by foreigners), waste is so bad in this country that the debt has ballooned to $36 trillion in just 4 years.

2. Kamala will rid America of gangs that have become so powerful. (In the last 4 years of Biden/Kamala America has more transnational gangs than ever before as represented by the murders in Chicago and other main cities and the biggest gangs of all are the cartels feasting on America's open border, which have made it easy for new gangs to come into the country and establish themselves. The cartels especially). In Colorado there is now a gang from Venezuela that is vicious and attacking people. NYC has a major gang problem now originating from illegal migrants.

3. Stood up to powerful corporate interests (Google is still living high on a basis where no one else can compete, Facebook and Amazon are living high after

Biden took action during the pandemic that closed many small businesses eliminating competition for the big boys). The powerful corporate interests are in large measure supporting Democrats.

Chapter 15
Two major issues for Walz

Two major issues arose that tested Mr. Walz ability to govern in 2020 and 2021 – COVID and the George Floyd riots.

First, the COVID pandemic struck in 2020. Walz took a very strong stand on the pandemic, closing schools, churches, stores, etc. He declared a state of emergency on March 25, 2020, and ruled by decree for 15 months. He proclaimed the emergency on the basis of an allegedly sophisticated Minnesota Model projection of the virus's course in the state. In fact, the projection reflected a weekend's work by graduate students at the University of Minnesota School of Public Health. Relying on their research, Mr. Walz presented a scenario in which an estimated 74,000 Minnesotans would perish from the virus. The following week the Star Tribune reported that with the lockdown Mr. Walz ordered, 50,000 would die. Maybe it would have been preferable to address the virus through democratic means.

16,135 was Minnesota's total death number for COVID, a bit lower than Walz model of 74,000, 4 ½ times more than actual. Was this purposeful to shock the people or was it just a very poor estimate with inadequate research? To change the lives of so many in a negative way with such inadequate research is unforgiveable. The 74,000 number panicked Minnesotans and caused untold amounts of misery and loss in suicides, mental conditions, divorces, lost businesses, loss of group worship, loss of almost 2 years of education, and many Christian acts of charity and growth.

What is a Democrat?

I visited Minnesota during the pandemic and was amazed how frightened everyone was. Some wouldn't open their door if you knocked. The government and media had truly scared many Minnesotans. I wonder how the cost of closing down and the impact on people compares to the cost of the damage by COVID.

Mr. Walz took an extreme position which destroyed jobs and impeded life routines, including family get-togethers and church attendance. The biggest hit was closing schools and using the internet. Families with students lacking the skills and money to keep their child progressing on line or home schooling, lost essentially two years of education. An already digressing educational system fell precipitously in basic courses such as reading. It has been said by some education experts that this loss of education will never be made up and will affect their entire life. Recent test shows a dramatic drop in performance. See below.

Statewide, scores are down significantly since the beginning of the pandemic, which education officials say presented a challenge for students and teachers as schools closed and students shifted to remote or hybrid learning. Reading and math are both down 8.4 percentage points from 2019.

In St. Paul Public Schools, students' overall scores had little change from those of last year. St. Paul had terrible test scores on the basics of education. About 26% of students scored proficient in math, 34.1% were proficient in reading and 25.4% in science. The largest improvement from last year's proficiency scores came in science with an increase of only 1.4%, well within the margin of an estimate.

Church attendance was slow in recovering after having their doors closed for a significant amount of time. Where does the amendment separating church and state come in?

Many businesses were not able to open again. The lack of revenue for a long period of time was too much for many of them to handle. Ironically, the big stores such as Walmart, Target and Home Depot were allowed to stay open. Since their many departments were all in one store, they were able to sell things that their competition of smaller companies could not. So, while the small companies were going broke the big ones were basking in a less competitive market, thanks to government.

Mr. Walz finally let his one-man rule of COVID lapse on July 1, 2021. When the Johns Hopkins Coronavirus Resource Center stopped counting in March 2023, the Minnesota deaths were 14,870. None of these were school age children and people that shopped at the big stores that were opened seemed to be immune from COVID since most of the deaths were people who had basic health problems and could not handle the COVID virus with their current condition. As you might expect the elderly took the biggest hit.

Fraud crept into the picture in Minnesota especially. Minnesota led the nation in COVID fraud. Under the auspices of the Feeding Our Future nonprofit, its founder, Aimee Bock, allegedly recruited mostly young Somali men to seek reimbursement for millions of meals supposedly served to poor students and families. According to indictments handed up by a grand jury to U.S. Attorney Andrew Luger, Ms. Bock and others allegedly defrauded the state and federal government of $250 million.

In September 2022, Judge Guthmann authorized a news release titled "Correcting media reports and statements by Gov. Tim Walz concerning orders issued by the court." The release concluded: "As the public court record and Judge Guthmann's orders make plain, Judge Guthmann never issued an order requiring the MN Department of Education to resume food reimbursement payments to FOF. The Department of Education voluntarily resumed payments and informed the court that FOF resolved the 'serious deficiencies' that prompted it to suspend payments temporarily. All of the MN Department of Education food reimbursement payments to FOF were made voluntarily, without any court order."

Walz also signed a law in 2023 that created a universal school meals program that is now entering its second school year. While state leaders have applauded that success, they recently acknowledged free meals will cost a lot more than initially budgeted — $81 million more over the next two years and $95 million in the two years after that.

What is a Democrat?

The program is popular, but it's already costing the state more money than expected — the estimated price tag is about $480 million for the first two years. There is no detailed explanation of the added cost yet but as the pandemic fraud was unexpected, it is possible that fraud also is involved in the education food program.

The second item was the George Floyd event. He was murdered by a police man and set off protests nation-wide.

The George Floyd event was an event orchestrated by the Mayor of Minneapolis. He had a problem with policemen because he seemed to fully believe in the lie that everyone but Democrats are racists and I presume he assumed the policemen were white. Once he heard about the incident he immediately and publicly defined it as a racist act by racist policemen. The Mayor went ballistic informing the Democratic Party, Governor, Senator and most of all the media immediately blaming it on racism and the policemen. BLM was also called so the incident became one of America's greatest incidents involving the police and truthfully, the reaction was dramatically out of proportion.

The four policemen involved were fired within 24 hours with no investigation at the mayor's orders

The information that was never accurately reported was lost in the racist accusations that all the Democrats lived on. They felt this would be a terrific help to their next election. The MRT (Maximum Restraint Technique) that is a police extreme hold when the person is fighting arrest with every bone in his body, was not mentioned, Also the criminal action of Floyd was not clearly communicated. Floyds arrest history included according to court records in Harris County (Texas), which encompasses Floyd's hometown of Houston, nine arrests on nine separate occasions between 1997 and 2007, mostly on drug and theft charges that resulted in months-long jail sentences.

In regard to the Minneapolis attempted arrest the owner of the store was Mahmoud Abumayyaleh. He was not in the store. It was manned by a teenage clerk who had only been employed for six months. The clerk called 911because of Floyd's attempt to cash a counterfeit $20 bill. The owner said Floyd had been a regular customer for about a year, and he never caused any issues. Two MPD officers — Thomas Lane and J. A. Kueng — responded to the 911 call and, after talking to people inside the store, went to find Floyd in a parked vehicle nearby.

As Lane began speaking with Floyd, who was sitting in the driver's seat of the vehicle with Morries Hall his drug dealer, the officer pulled his gun out and instructed Floyd to show his hands. Floyd complied with the order, whereupon the officer holstered his gun. Then, Lane ordered Floyd out of the car and "put his hands on Floyd, and pulled him out of the car," and handcuffed him. Floyd walked with Lane to the sidewalk and sat on the ground at Lane's direction. When Mr. Floyd sat down, he said "thank you man" and was calm. In a conversation that lasted just under two minutes, Lane asked Mr. Floyd for his name and identification. Lane asked Mr. Floyd if he was "on anything" and noted there was foam at the edges of his mouth. Lane explained that he was arresting Mr. Floyd for passing counterfeit currency. Counterfeit $20 bills were stuffed between the seats inside the car.

At 8:14 p.m., Officers Lane and Kueng stood Mr. Floyd up and attempted to walk Mr. Floyd to their squad car. As the officers tried to put Mr. Floyd in their squad car, Mr. Floyd stiffened up and fell to the ground. Mr. Floyd told the officers that he was not resisting but did not want to get in the back seat because he was claustrophobic. At that point, two other officers — Derek Chauvin and Tou Thao — arrived at the scene and tried again to get Floyd into a squad car. While they attempted to do so, he began asserting that he could not breathe. Then, according to criminal charges against Chauvin, the officer pulled Floyd out of the squad car, and "Mr. Floyd went to the ground face down and still handcuffed." The complaint continues:

Officer Kueng held Mr. Floyd's back and Officer Lane held his legs. Officer Chauvin placed his left knee in the area of Mr. Floyd's head and neck. Mr. Floyd said, 'I can't breathe' multiple times and repeatedly said, 'Mama' and 'please,' as well. At one point, Mr. Floyd said 'I'm about to die.'

What is a Democrat?

Firstly, on May 29, 2020, court documents revealed the Hennepin County Medical Examiner's investigation into Floyd's death showed "no physical findings that support a diagnosis of traumatic asphyxiation," and that "potential intoxicants" and preexisting cardiovascular disease "likely contributed to his death".

According to the county's postmortem toxicology screening, he was intoxicated with fentanyl and had recently used methamphetamines (as well as other substances).

Mr. Walz jumped on the racist train but did not take any action to handle the growing protest. Protest is a kind word for what happened. An emergency situation was sounded. Walz took a very calm almost indifferent position during one of the worst protests ever.

During the state of emergency, protests broke out in Minneapolis on Memorial Day 2020 following the death of George Floyd. That Thursday, rioters burned Minneapolis's Third Precinct police station to the ground. Although the mayor of Minneapolis cried for help when his police force was overrun, Mr. Walz, who took a very calm indifferent position did not respond to his request for the national guard until the weekend. In just three days, riots, arson and looting throughout the Twin Cities caused $500 million in property damage, burned down 150 buildings, destroyed 350 businesses, and killed three people. That could have been much less had Mr. Walz responded in a timely fashion so you might say the Governor was responsible for much of the damage caused by the protests. Governor Walz in his campaign for VP a few years later stated that the protesters were Americans enjoying their freedoms and no harm was done.

As a result of the George Floyd event, the City Council and Mayor defunded the police and called for changes. The council consisted of 12 Democrats and 1 Green Party candidate. The unfriendly signals from Mayors office, prompted policemen to take early retirement and some to change to cities that treated their policemen with respect. Minneapolis quickly was short 22% in policemen and crime soared. In one year, they had 600 car jackings.

In 2023 they even achieved the #1 position of all American cities in crime. St. Paul was number 2.

I confronted Mr. Walz one morning at a breakfast meeting where he was speaking. He acknowledged that the first responsibility of government is safety of their citizens but had no constructive plans as was verified by his subsequent large amounts of extra expenditures on everything but the police. Safety of citizens does not seem to be a high priority with Governor Walz.

The accusation that the police were racists and caused the incident prompted Ocasio-Cortex and other left wing Democrats to say that police shootings are the leading cause of death for young men and if they are Black even greater risk.

But to prove the falsehood of what was said by some Democrats, the Washington Post printed some statistics about black murders:

- In 2019, among all black men between the ages of 18 and 29, 103 were fatally shot by police. Out of the 103, 99 of them were armed.
- The FBI reported that 2,906 black or African American males were tragically killed by other civilians in 2019.
- Of those 2,906 murders, 2,574 were killed by Black offenders (9 out of 10).

Thus, the Democrat's racism accusation that is used daily is purely a campaign strategy.

The family of George Floyd was awarded $27 million.

The above story is mostly from a book by Liz Collin who worked for WCCO alongside Don Shelby, one of the most popular news reporters in Minnesota. Her husband was the president of the police union and deeply involved in the George Floyd story. Because she was married to Bob, a policeman, she was included in the attack by protestors which included death threats, pinata effigies, and demonstrations outside the studio and police union. They both had to leave their jobs.

It seems to me that Chauvin overreacted to George Floyd's

situation that appears to be related to his vascular condition and the drugs he took but the mistake was not worthy of the hysteria that caused the damage done in all our cities, the lives lost in the protests and thereafter in the black community. Also Chauvin had a history of over powering suspects that were uncooperative and management of Chauvin was certainly an issue..

Chapter 16
Walz gains control of Minnesota

After taking office in 2019, Gov. Walz was restrained by a one-seat Republican majority in the state Senate—until In November 2022 Mr. Walz was elected to a second term, and the DFL won majorities in both chambers of the Legislature. In the preceding two years the state had accumulated an $18 billion budget surplus. With the DFL in full control, Mr. Walz and the Legislature increased the budget for 2024 to 2025 from 60 billion to 72 billion. They only returned $1 billion of the $18 billion surplus enabling them to spend big in the 2024-2025 season.

1. Taxes:He raised taxes in as many areas as he could and at the end of 2023 though out his first term even accumulated a surplus of $18 billion. Many clamored for a refund but Walz had other plans. He wanted to be Santa Claus at the expense of the taxpayers. He only accommodated them by refunding $1 billion. The rest he used on the next budget that increased from $60 billion to $72 billion. At the same time, he instituted numerous expensive projects, and extra spending on his favorite items, education being one. Cities and counties followed raising or installing sales taxes. Now in St. Paul there is a state, county and city sales tax.

2. Major increases were made especially on education due in part to feeding all students both breakfast and lunch. They have also raised taxes at have some of the counties and cities.

Mr. Walz is unabashedly a socialist. He even stated, "Don't ever shy away from our progressive values. One person's socialism is another person's neighborliness." Note he doesn't mention the cost of socialism and the reduction in freedom.

Socialism tends to also use government control for moral issues and Mr. Walz certainly accomplished that.

Chapter 17
Abortion and Transgender Rules

The most controversial moral issue today is abortion and that has become one of the leading special interest groups for Democrats. Abortion is the panacea for Mr. Walz with his DFL colleagues. They have backed measures establishing Minnesota as a mecca for abortion and a "trans refuge." The legislation prohibits enforcing out-of-state subpoenas, arrest warrants and extradition requests for people from other states who seek treatment that is legal in Minnesota. Below is a list of the extreme pro-abortion laws passed immediately upon the 2024 term with Democrat majorities in the House and Senate.

1. Legal abortions for all nine months, for any reason, right up to birth.
2. Legislation increasing taxpayer support for Medicaid-funded abortions in Minnesota.
3. Elimination of laws requiring medical care for babies that survive abortion attempts on their lives.
4. He actively targeted and eliminated Minnesota's "Positive Alternatives" program, which provided funding to pregnancy centers in the state.

It was Gov. Tim Walz who escorted and campaigned with Kamala Harris for the first time ever (for any VP) at a Planned parenthood in Minnesota. Yet, he actively targeted and eliminated Minnesota's

"Positive Alternatives" program, which provided funding to pregnancy centers in the state. Proving Mr. Walz prioritizes and supports one choice – more abortions, not alternative resources to help mothers and babies. Because Pro-Lifers created pregnancy centers as an alternative to abortion by meeting the needs of mothers with unplanned pregnancies, especially those facing pressure or coercion. Most people who love life more than convenience even by a death alternative, love and support pregnancy centers.

Mr. Walz exposed his hypocrisy on women's rights when he purposefully got rid of Minnesota's law forbidding women to be coerced into having abortions. He even repealed the requirement that women must be given informed consent – *any* consent – to an abortion. As national Review puts it, "Under Tim Walz", Minnesota went from a pro-choice state to a radically pro-abortion state at the expense of pregnant women."

The transgender community has recently become a new special interest group for Democrats and the idea of children being authorized for hormone treatments or surgery to alter sex characteristics is mostly banned if not done with parent's consent. Gov. Walz came on board the transgender bandwagon by setting laws that bars complying with court orders issued in other states to remove children from their parents' custody. Children can now order sex change surgery that could be nonreversible. Considering the immaturity of children especially in an atmosphere of transgender peers are subject to making a wrong decision which can make their life difficult forever.

Mr. Walz was also on board with men competing in women sports by claiming a sex change, which of course had nothing to do with their male size and strength. He has been very vocal in allowing men claiming a sex change to compete with women. Mr. Walz ignores the inherent strength of males as detailed by Journal of Strength and Conditioning Research. "Male subjects become notably stronger than female subjects around age 15 years. In adults, sex differences in strength are more pronounced in upper-body than lower-body muscles and in concentric than eccentric contractions.

John Benedict

Greater male than female strength is not because of higher voluntary activation but to greater muscle mass and type II fiber areas. Men participate in strength training more frequently than women. Men are motivated more by challenge, competition, social recognition, and a desire to increase muscle size and strength. Men also have greater preference for competitive, high-intensity, and upper-body exercise. Women are motivated more by improved attractiveness, muscle "toning," and body mass management."

And Mr. Walz picked up a nickname, *Tampon Tim,* for putting Tampons in the men's latrine at schools.

Chapter 18
Managing Taxpayer Money

A big issue with the governor is his *management of taxpayer's money*. There are two very large fraud crimes committed against Minnesota that cost the taxpayers enormous amounts of money and big losses on the building and operation of light rails. Billions have been lost and no correction is imminent. Attempts are being made to prosecute some of the fraud criminals but no doubt that will never recover the losses due to fraud;

1. The Minneapolis nonprofit received millions from the US Department of Agriculture over nearly two years under relaxed pandemic-era rules to quickly bring food to the needy. Only a small amount was spent as intended, prosecutors said. The ghost program was outed in a series of Justice Department indictments in late 2022, after Walz and his administration kowtowed to politically connected nonprofit groups while ignoring fraud warnings from local whistleblowers — and never checking on the charity's inflated numbers and blatantly fake filings. Just like his fictitious meals fraud, the citizens of Minnesota lost over $250 million.

2. June 13, 2024 a U. S. attorney announced that Minnesota had the greatest pandemic fraud of any

state, something just under $300 million. This money was part of the COVID relief scheme.

3. The nature and scale of the fraud are staggering. Mr. Walz tried to blame state district court judge John Guthmann, who in April 2021 handled a case regarding the department's processing of applications for reimbursements. According to Mr. Walz, Judge Guthmann ordered the state to continue payouts to the alleged perpetrators of the fraud even after the state Education Department discovered it. Walz's appointees at the state Department of Education "created opportunities for fraud" thanks to their totally "inadequate oversight" and ignored "warning signs" about Feeding Our Future even before the pandemic, a Minnesota legislative audit revealed.

4. For Walz breakfast and lunch program for all students, the Minnesota Department of Education oversaw the payout of more than $490 million for two years, more than double what they expected. Considering the fraud on the pandemic, it is entirely possible that fraud was also involved in this program. As I cite later, the Walz administration has not been good at qualifying and monitoring expenditures of large amounts of money.

5. "Minnesota has a mismatch between the entities that fund the construction of light rail transit projects and the entities responsible for constructing them," wrote the Office of the Legislative Auditor in a special report requested by the Legislature. "We also found that the Metropolitan Council obligated itself to spend money it did not have, added or changed substantial work after the project was bid, and was not fully transparent about the project's increasing costs and delays."

What is a Democrat?

6. But while the report brought no new revelations, having it all in one place by an independent auditor was sobering for members of the joint Legislative Audit Commission.

7. The Metropolitan Council bungled oversight of the construction of the Southwest Light Rail by failing to enforce its agreements with its contractors, adding hundreds of millions of dollars to the project's cost and causing further delays, according to a report by the Office of the Legislative Auditor released Wednesday.

8. The 14.5-mile project from Target Field to Eden Prairie was supposed to cost $2 billion and carry its first passengers in 2023 when it was approved by the federal government in 2018. It is now set to open in 2027 and cost $2.767 billion with the council not sure where all of the money is going to come from. Audit project manager David Kirshner described that 38% cost increase as "quite unusual" when compared to light rail projects across the U.S. Metro area. That represents a high level of incompetence at the government level who choses and pays the contractors.

9. Imagine committing to such a gigantic project and being off so far on dollars and schedule. Not only is the overage in construction out of reasonable expectations but operation of the light rails installed to date are grossly under paid by riders. Walz has promoted the light rail with billions of dollars and neglected to create a means of collecting fees from each individual as they board.

10. The rails were installed with no method to collect fees so many of the riders do not pay. They now have

to police that activity which of course is just a spot check and very ineffective.

11. Secondly the light rails have become an opportunity for crime. Many young criminals ride the light rails for free while they rob, assault and worse right on the rails. Many have given up riding on the rails or only ride at safe times. Light Rail provided less than a third of total rides but more than half the total number of crimes systemwide, according to Metro Transit data for 2021 and 2022. As ridership has slowly come back, crime has risen. The Lake Street LRT station spiraled from 312 incidents in 2021 to 696 last year and 868 in the first eight months 2023.

12. The light rail system is a major example of Walz's disinterest in managing the taxpayer's money.

I think it would be fair to say that governor Walz does not place the management of taxpayer's money at the top of his agenda.

How would we summarize the socialistic actions of Mr. Walz?

First of all, he is in the front lines for the government to provide for people. He pretends that he is Santa Claus. For example, the food at the schools is the responsibility of parents and Mr. Walz is making that the responsibility of the taxpayers. It takes away personal responsibility that is necessary for freedom. That action is also intended to make citizens dependent on the government which allows the government to control them, thereby losing freedom. Feeding hungry children is an excellent idea but not an educational function. Feeding all children with taxpayer money instead of by parents who are fully capable is full socialism. Think about the many families who are living pay check to pay check and having a very difficult time paying the rent with the 20% inflation in the last four years helping to pay for food for many students that have parents who are millionaires. That is a good example of socialism reducing freedom and increasing the cost of government.

What is a Democrat?

He spends enormous amounts of money irresponsibly. The pandemic fraud case, the enormous new expense for school meals, the totally out of bounds expenditure for light rail with no means of collecting fees show a total lack of qualification and monitoring, basic actions when handling money. This spending is done mostly without the approval of taxpayers. Mr. Walz acts as if the money is his and he can do with it what he wants. He is not the owner but the steward who needs to be even more responsible than one would be with one's own money.

There is a total neglect of managing government expenditures.

Freedom is taken away when the government becomes an authority for moral values such as in the case of abortion and transgender activities. Those who believe otherwise (which are close to the 50% mark) receive no consideration even to the point of preventing pregnancy centers, an extremely egregious action.

Chapter 19
Democratic Strategy

Special Interest; the Democrats exist on special interest groups. I count over 25 of them. Recently they have gone to great lengths to capture illegal immigrants, prisoners, students with education loans, the LBQ special interest and the transgender special interest.

They are great marketers because they can connect with two special interest that are opposing each other. Examples;

- Catholics and pro-abortion
- Blacks and unions
- Christians and transgender
- Teachers and suburban housewives

Also, their primary focus in government seems to be buying votes (seeking legislation that is a reward for that special interest). For example, Biden has been trying to pay student loans throughout his tenure in the White House. There are $1.6 trillion of student loans. If we paid those off, we would add that to our massive debt and create a very difficult problem for those who worked their way through college. They would want and deserve equal economic support. Paying off student loans could then become a massive protest requesting retroactive payment back for decades. Also of course it would mean that all future education will be paid by the government. The effort to pay off student loans could multiply into a volcano.

One must also consider the reasons why some students can't

or won't pay off their loans. Some of them are:
- Less than 60% of students that attend a 4-year college graduate. Less than 20% of students attending a 2-year community college graduate. Those who didn't finish what they started are a large part of those not paying back their loans.
- Only 50.2% of 4-year graduates have full time jobs in the degree that they received. Once again, their failure is the reason they don't have the money to repay the loan. Why should taxpayers pay for their failures?
- Their degree did not offer them a job sufficient to pay their loan
- Their grades were such that they are not able to find a good paying job
- They are living a life style beyond their means. This is by far the biggest reason.

Spending taxpayer money to acquire votes poses a major problem for many Americans who want the government to make America stronger, use sound financial management so we don't have a $36 trillion debt, save money aimed at special interest for those in need – the sick, children without parents, mentally ill, homeless, widows, veterans, etc. America's purpose for voting is to make America better, not worse by accumulating more debt.

An interesting perspective of the Democrats super attention to special interest. What often is not good for America may not even be good for the special interest. Note the three largest special interests of Democrats and the results:

1. The Teachers Union is very loyal and provides a major if not the top revenue for election campaigns. Yet America, although they spend by far the most

on education of any country in the world ranks as 31rst according to a worldwide test. The Teachers are apparently very content with Democrats but education results are extremely poor according to a worldwide testing survey. Is education about pleasing teachers and Democrats or parents.

2. The black population won over with the War on Poverty giving black women money so they do not need a husband has resulted in many black children not even knowing who their father is and without a father they often follow a life of crime, unemployment and a lack of education. Only about four-in-ten Black people in the U.S. (39) live in households that are headed by married couples as of 2022. Black children living only with their mother is almost twice that of any other group. Among Black U.S. households in 2022, 49% earned less than $50,000, while 51% made $50,000 or more. A third of Black households (34%) earned $75,000 or more, including 22% that made $100,000 or more. These income numbers are by far the worse of any group.

3. Cities are predominantly Democratic. For example, Minneapolis has 12 Democrats and one Green Party on the City Council headed by a Democratic mayor. They have severe crime and educational problems. The Twin Cities are just like all the cities governed by Democrats.

4. Pharmaceutical industry is the second largest lobbying group. They have persuaded congress and the white House to allow a flood of pharmaceuticals, some very expensive. The biggest result of pharmaceutical lobbying is that unlike other countries,

What is a Democrat?

the government does not negotiate prices based on volume. Often, pharmaceuticals manipulate prices by introducing new drugs very much like their old ones but having a patent so they can sell at much higher prices. Pharmaceuticals have been known to buy out a competitor who is selling a drug not protected by patent so that they have an exclusive enabling much higher prices to be used.

5. Some very expensive drugs are available now. In December 2021, Danyelza increased in price 3.5%, bringing the cost of a single vial to $21,081. People typically use around 48 vials per year, bringing the annual cost close to $1,011,882.

The FDA's primary responsibility is to protect the citizens of America. They totally failed in approving *OxyContin*, the drug that helped steer the country into an opioid epidemic that has killed almost half a million people the last two decades.

There are other drugs that have done much damage but on a smaller scale. However, the drug companies have found a way to be immune to responsibility. They convinced the FDA that a warning on the label when drugs are dangerous is sufficient to protect the patient leaving the pharmaceuticals free and clear. Making the judgment that a patient who might be sick but certainly without knowledge about drugs can understand the label and find the energy to decide not to use it based upon the warning. If everyone read the warning and chose not to use it there would be no market so the concept of a warning label is insane if you really want a patient to protect themselves from the drug manufacturer. My neighbor went blind and then found that Statin has that side effect, very rarely but sometimes. Although the Statin manufacturers sell $20 billion a year, they did not take responsibility for my neighbor going blind.

In spite of being by far the largest user of medication in the world, our longevity is an embarrassing 30th of all the countries.

Chapter 20
History of Democratic Presidents

One very revealing way to describe the Democratic Party is to look at the Democratic presidents and track how they evolved into a democratic president of the 21rst century. The Democratic Party was founded in 1828 as an outgrowth of the Anti-Federalist Party, there have been 16 Democrats as president of the United States.

America's first seven presidents were neither Democrats nor Republicans. First president George Washington, who detested the very idea of partisan politics, belonged to no party. John Adams, our second president, was a Federalist, America's first political party. Third through sixth presidents Thomas Jefferson, James Madison, James Monroe, and John Quincy Adams were all members of the Democratic-Republican Party, which later splintered to become the modern Democratic Party and the Whig Party.

Andrew Jackson (7th President)
Cited as the founder of the Democratic Party, his version was nothing like today. Elected in 1828 and again in 1832. In the War of 1812, he was a general and later became the seventh president. Andrew Jackson served two terms lasting from 1829 to 1837.

True to the philosophy of the new Democratic Party, Jackson advocated protecting "natural rights" against the attacks of a "corrupt aristocracy." With distrust of sovereign rule still running hot, this platform appealed to the American people, who swept him to a landslide victory in 1828 over incumbent John Quincy Adams.

Martin Van Buren (8th President)

In 1812 Van Buren ran for a seat in the New York Senate; on the campaign trail, he opposed a strong federal government. Van Buren developed a reputation as a gifted politician, and his skill was apparent when he created the Albany Regency, an informal political organization in New York state that was a prototype of the modern political machine. It became a powerful force in state politics. He was known as the "Little Magician" to his friends (and the "Sly Fox" to his enemies) in recognition of his reputed cunning and skill as a politician.

James K, Polk (11th President)

Serving one term from 1845 to 1849, President Polk was an advocate of Andrew Jackson's "common man" democracy. Polk remains the only president to have served as Speaker of the House.

Though considered a dark-horse in the 1844 election, Polk defeated Whig Party candidate Henry Clay in a nasty campaign. Polk's support for U.S. annexation of the Republic of Texas, considered a key to western expansion and Manifest Destiny, proved popular with voters.

Franklin Pierce (14th President)

Serving a single term, from 1853 to 1857, 14th President Franklin Pierce was a Northern Democrat who considered the abolitionist movement the greatest threat to national unity.

As president, Pierce's aggressive enforcement of the Fugitive Slave Act angered the growing number of anti-slavery voters. Today, many historians and scholars contend that the failure of his pro-slavery policies to halt secession and prevent the Civil War make Pierce one of America's worst and least effective presidents.

James Buchanan (15th President)

Fifteenth President James Buchanan served from 1857 to 1861 and had previously served as Secretary of State and as a member of the House and Senate.

Elected just before the Civil War, Buchanan inherited—but mostly failed to address—the issues of slavery and secession. After his election, he angered Republican abolitionists and Northern Democrats alike by supporting the Supreme Court's Dred Scott v. Sandford ruling and siding with southern lawmakers in their attempts to admit Kansas to the Union as a pro-slavery state. James Buchanan continued the pro slavery issue as did all of the southern Democrats. As United states expanded to the north and west, the south lost the majorities in the Senate which they knew would lead to an anti-slavery congress. This made the 1860 election crucial to them. when they lost the election by a great deal of votes, the south knew that they only had two choices – to give up on slavery or to secede from the union.

Andrew Johnson (17th President)
Considered one of the worst U.S. presidents, 17th President Andrew Johnson served from 1865 to 1869.

Johnson was elected vice president to Republican Abraham Lincoln on the post-Civil War reconstruction period National Union ticket; he assumed the presidency after Lincoln was assassinated.

Although Johnson was on the ticket with a Republican anti-slavery Lincoln, he was still a Democrat and very open to slavery. Lincoln's assassination extended black servitude for another 100 years. Although this was paid servitude, blacks still had few voting rights or impact on the state government. As president, Johnson's refusal to ensure the protection of formerly enslaved people from potential federal prosecution resulted in his impeachment by the Republican-dominated House of Representatives. Though he was acquitted in the Senate by one vote, Johnson never ran for reelection.

Grover Cleveland (22nd and 24th President)
As the only president ever elected to two non-consecutive terms, 22nd and 24th President Grover Cleveland served from 1885 to 1889 and from 1893 to 1897.

His pro-business policies and demand for fiscal conservatism won Cleveland the support of both Democrats and Republicans. However, his inability to reverse the depression of the Panic of 1893 decimated the Democratic Party and set the stage for a Republican landslide in the 1894 mid-term congressional election.

Cleveland would be the last Democrat to win the presidency until the 1912 election of Woodrow Wilson.

Woodrow Wilson (28th President)
Elected in 1912 after 23 years of Republican dominance, 28th Democratic president Woodrow Wilson would serve two terms from 1913 to 1921.

Along with leading the nation during World War I, Wilson drove the enactment of progressive social reform legislation, the likes of which would not be seen again until Franklin Roosevelt's New Deal of 1933.

Issues facing the nation at the time of Wilson's election included the question of women's suffrage, which he opposed, calling it a matter for the states to decide.

Franklin D. Roosevelt (32nd President)
Elected to an unprecedented and now constitutionally impossible four terms, 32nd President Franklin D. Roosevelt (FDR) served from 1933 until his death in 1945.

Widely considered one of the greatest presidents, people believe that Roosevelt led the United States through no less desperate crises than the Great Depression during his first two terms and World War II during his last two. However, another view taints that scenario.

Roosevelt took America in its first big step to socialism. In an attempt to recover from the severe recession of 1932, he instituted

What is a Democrat?

government programs to put people back to work. As usual the attempt to spend our way out of the recession was not as successful as many people thought. Even in 1937, the country descended to an economic crisis comparable to the 1932 crisis. Roosevelt had to change his rules and legislation that caused this crisis to save America once again from a terrible economic disaster, this time created by him.

The recession never really recovered until WW II. The war became a manufacturing miracle to produce weapons not just for America but for our allies who were essentially in the front lines. European factories were more susceptible to being bombed.

Today, Roosevelt's depression-ending New Deal Package of social reform programs is considered the prototype for American Liberalism.

Roosevelt's leadership in WWII is controversial. He failed to alert Pearl Harbor about the eminent danger from Japan, that had been growing. Japan and the United States had been discussing a meeting to agree in principle on major issues such as Japan's intervention in China. There needed to be preliminary agreements to get to that point. On Dec. 6, Japan basically closed the door to preliminary meetings and therefore it was essentially an announcement that Japan would continue their aggression and since United States stood in the way, we were very likely a target for them. In a crucial meeting between the Japanese ambassador and the secretary of state, the Japanese refused to go forward culminating in a disagreement in Washington immediately before Pearl Harbor was attacked. Instead of immediately advising the military in Hawaii of the upcoming Japanese attacks, the information was sent by snail mail arriving a few hours after the attack.

Roosevelt's association with Stalin overrode Winston's Churchill's caution to the point where Roosevelt even met separately with Stalin at times. That ultimately gave Russia Eastern Europe for over 50 years resulting in communist domination taking away individual freedom and progress for hundreds of millions of Europeans.

Finally, Roosevelt became frail and sick even though elected to a fourth term. His responsibility was so great he should not have continued with such failing health. He died in April of 1945 allowing a healthy Truman to end the war and bring America back into an economy no longer fed by the needs of war.

Harry S. Truman (33rd President)
Perhaps best known for his decision to end World War II by dropping atomic bombs on the Japanese cities of Hiroshima and Nagasaki, 33rd president Harry S. Truman took office upon the death of Franklin D. Roosevelt and served from 1945 to 1953.

Despite famous headlines erroneously announcing his defeat, Truman defeated Republican Thomas Dewey in the 1948 election. As president, Truman faced the Korean War, the emerging threat of communism, and the start of the Cold War. Truman's domestic policy marked him as a moderate Democrat whose liberal legislative agenda resembled Franklin Roosevelt›s New Deal.

Truman led a different approach to managing the revival of the enemy countries of Germany, Italy and Japan. Unlike the harsh treatment of 1919, the enemy was helped to form a democracy and get back on their feet. This was a huge success unlike what Russia did to Eastern Europe.

Harry Truman responded to the attempt by North Korea to expand its communist reach by capturing South Korea. South Korea was unable to protect itself so the United States sent the military to Korea to defend South Korea. The war was successful until China decided to support North Korea and that gradually brought the war to an end with no success by North Korea or the United States. This seemed to be a prelude to Vietnam. A war costing the lives of over 36,000 Americans and 3 million civilians and military participants for nothing. The boundary was essentially the same after the war as before. This is so typical of some wars.

John F. Kennedy (35th President)
Popularly known as JFK, John F. Kennedy served as 35th president from 1961 until his assassination in November 1963.

Serving at the height of the Cold War, JFK spent much of his time in office dealing with relations with the Soviet Union, highlighted by the tense atomic diplomacy of the 1962 Cuban Missile Crisis. Kennedy showed great toughness and wisdom in forcing the USSR to take their missiles out of Cuba. Bobby Kennedy, John's brother was very active in his position as attorney general. He went after the mafia and sought freedom for the blacks in the South.

Calling it the "New Frontier," Kennedy's domestic program promised greater funding for education, medical care for the elderly, economic aid to rural areas, and an end to racial discrimination.

In addition, JFK officially launched America into the "Space Race" with the Soviets, culminating with the Apollo 11 moon landing in 1969.

Lyndon B. Johnson (36th President)
Assuming the office after the assassination of John F. Kennedy, 36th President Lyndon B. Johnson served from 1963 to 1969.

While much of his time in office was spent defending his often controversial role in the escalation of U.S. involvement in the Vietnam War, Johnson succeeded in passing legislation first conceived in President Kennedy's "New Frontier" plan.

Johnson's "Great Society" program, consisted of social reform legislation protecting civil rights, prohibiting racial discrimination, and expanding programs like Medicare, Medicaid, and support for education and the arts. Johnson is also remembered for his "War on Poverty" program, which created jobs and helped millions of Americans overcome poverty. The war on poverty also enabled black women to live and bear children without a husband. That cemented Democrats with the black vote for decades as Johnson predicted. However, it also made fathers obsolete so men became irresponsible Romeos robbing children of a father. Today in much of the cities, 80% of black children do not know who their father is. Fathers of course provide discipline and leadership. With out them, we have a great deal of crime and a lack of motivation by young men.

The civil rights act of 1965 was passed only because of the Republican votes. The majority of Democrats voted against the bill. Republicans are often called racist by Democrats but the governance by the Democrats first held them to slavery, then paid servants and with the Civil Rights Act destroyed many black families. Today in the cities that are dominated by Democratic politicians, the black population still suffers from crime, a deficient education system and jobs. That would make anyone question who is racist.

LBJ also set a precedent by being the first to use social security money for his other programs. Up until that time Social Security was well funded but quickly became an oft used resource to pay government extravagance.

LBJ's management of the Vietnam war was ineffective. We never attempted to win; a precedent introduced by the North Korean war. That did not stop the death of more than **3 million people** (including over 58,000 Americans). More than half of the dead were Vietnamese civilians. With the war dragging on for years, the country grew tired of the deaths and the protests. LBJ knew he could not win another term so he dropped out.

Jimmy Carter (39th President)
The son of a successful Georgia peanut farmer, Jimmy Carter served as 39th president from 1977 to 1981.

As his first official act, Carter granted presidential pardons to all Vietnam War-era military draft evaders. He also oversaw the creation of two new cabinet-level federal departments, the Department of Energy and the Department of Education. Having specialized in nuclear power while in the Navy, Carter ordered the creation of America's first national energy policy and pursued the second round of Strategic Arms Limitation Talks. Jimmy Carter was a detailed man and often missed the bigger picture because of his habit to nitpick details. The education department has proven to be nothing more than an employment agency and a user of $90 billion in 2024. The original budget was $12 billion. Education has become a bureaucracy creating many socialistic avenues. Education in America is worse today than when the department was started. America ranks 31rst in the world.

Under Carter, inflation set a record of 9.9% per year. Interest rate on mortgages grew to 13%. Prices on many items increased every few months. Harold Volcker during Reagan's term took painful steps to stop the inflation and it worked. By contrast under Trump the inflation was 1.9% per year.

In foreign policy, Carter escalated the Cold War by ending détente. Near the end of his single term, Carter was faced by the 1979-1981 Iran hostage crisis and the international boycott of the 1980 Summer Olympics in Moscow. Carter boycotted the Olympics in the USSR because of his dissatisfaction with the USSR's actions in Afghanistan and the violations of human rights.

Carter also arranged a treaty between Arafat representing Palestinians and Israel, called the Camp David accord. The treaty was hailed but terrorist's actions never fully stopped and Arafat personally profited from the Camp David Accord. Other attempts by Clinton to bring peace to a Palestinian society called the Oslo Agreement was of little help. Palestinians were never about to accept Israel's possession of the land once settled by Muslims even though before that by Jews.

Jimmy Carter is regarded by many as one of our worst presidents because of enormous inflation and weakness overseas that fueled Iran's conversion to Muslim extremism and the kidnapping of the US embassy in Tehran. 52 of the embassy staff were held for 444 days, only released when Reagan was about to be inaugurated. Carter attempted a surprise military rescue on April 24, 1980, an ill-fated military operation to rescue the American hostages held in Tehran. This operation ended with eight U.S. servicemen dead and no hostages rescued. This was one of the worst presidential debacles ever but not as bad as Biden's Afghan evacuation debacle. With the Iran Hostage Crisis stretching into its sixth month and all diplomatic appeals to the Iranian government ending in failure, President Jimmy Carter ordered the military mission as a last ditch attempt to save the hostages. During the operation, three of eight helicopters failed, crippling the crucial airborne plans. The mission was then canceled at the staging area in Iran, but during the withdrawal one of the retreating helicopters collided with one of six C-130 transport planes, killing eight service members and injuring five. The next day, a somber Jimmy Carter gave a press conference in which he took full responsibility for the tragedy. The hostages were not released for another 270 days just before Reagan was inaugurated. The Iranians knew that Reagan would take immediate military action unlike Jimmy Carter.

Bill Clinton (42nd President)

Former Arkansas governor Bill Clinton served two terms as the 42nd president from 1993 to 2001. Considered a centrist, Clinton attempted to create policies that balanced conservative and liberal philosophies.

Along with welfare reform legislation, he drove the creation of the State Children's Health Insurance Program. In 1998, the House of Representatives voted to impeach Clinton on charges of perjury and obstruction of justice relating to his admitted affair with White House intern Monica Lewinsky.

Acquitted by the Senate in 1999, Clinton went on to complete his second term during which the government recorded its first budget surplus since 1969. This surplus was the result of Clinton raising taxes in his first two years and the Republicans taking over congress in 1994 and reducing spending. The best of both Partys at work.

In foreign policy, Clinton ordered U.S. military intervention in Bosnia and Kosovo and signed the Iraq Liberation Act in opposition to Saddam Hussein.

Clinton also tried to follow Carter's lead in resolving the Palestinian- Israel issues with the Oslo Agreement. That too resulted in more hope than improvements.

However, Clinton, like Carter was timid at times costing many lives. He did not pursue Osama Bin Laden aggressively when attacks were made against the US military. Eventually that led to the destruction of the world Trade Centers and almost 3000 lives.

He also did not stop the Rwanda wars that cost 1 million lives. America could have stopped those wars in an instant. Ironically, many called Clinton the black president because of his openness to them but in the case of Rwanda, there was no action. Clinton later confessed that he made a mistake.

Bill Clinton with his partner Hillary left the white House broke but within 15 years had taken in more than $240 million. Bill made much of the money including $189 million writing books, giving speeches, consulting private companies and advising billionaires. His speeches netted $106 million. This speech net was enhanced a great deal by countries buying speeches while doing business with Hillary Clinton, the current Secretary of State.

Barack Obama (44th President)

The first Black president elected to the office; Barack Obama served two terms as 44th president from 2009 to 2017. While best remembered for "Obamacare," the Patient Protection and Affordable Care Act, Obama signed many landmark bills into law. This included the American Recovery and Reinvestment Act of 2009, intended to bring the nation out of the Great Recession of 2008. Obama followed Roosevelt's design for recovering from a recession, buying our way out. As with Roosevelt, the recovery slowed and the debt was increased about $10 trillion.

Obamacare added a great deal of bureaucracy to our medical health system and did not improve health. America spends 50% more per person on health than the second most expensive country and our longevity is only rated 30th in the world.

In foreign policy, Obama ended U.S. military involvement in the Iraq War but increased U.S. troop levels in Afghanistan. In addition, he orchestrated a reduction of nuclear weapons with the United States-Russia New START treaty.

Obama followed the timidity of Carter and Clinton. His lack of effort failed in ridding the Middle East of the terrorist group ISIS. ISIS was still strong but Trump eradicated ISIS in a matter of months.

Obama released Iran from the financial sanctions that the United States had, releasing them to further support terrorists. His red line warning to Russia and Syria not to use chemical weapons especially against Syrian civilians was not backed up. When Russia seized Crimea from Ukraine, Obama did not take any effective action and that ultimately caused Russia to make the effort to seize Ukraine choosing a weak democratic President in both instance when the seizure was made.

In his second term, Obama issued executive orders requiring fair and equal treatment of LGBTQ+ people in the U.S. and lobbied the Supreme Court to strike down state laws banning same-sex marriage.

Obama followed Clinton's path. In only 8 years he increased his net worth to $70 million after he left the White House. His income was primarily from books, movies and even audible programs. He also invested wisely.

Joe Biden (46th President)
The former vice president to Barack Obama, Joe Biden was elected to the presidency to serve a term beginning in 2021. Before serving as Obama's vice president, Biden was a senator representing Delaware in the U.S. Senate from 1973 to 2009; at the time of his first election, he was the sixth-youngest senator in history, winning his first election at only 29 years old.

Biden's career in the Senate included controversial causes such as the Comprehensive Crime Control Act (1984) and opposition to race-integration busing. However, he also led the way for major victories such as the Violence Against Women Act. As vice president, he gained a reputation for raising questions that no one else would and looking at issues from different angles. He led the justice committee during the Bork nomination that began the strong partisanship that has prevailed to this day. Biden worked very hard to stop the Bork nomination. Since that time, we have had some strong partisan battles during the nomination process. Some of the battles are contrived and distorted even trying to dig up dirt when the nominee was in High School.

Upon beginning his presidential term, Biden's priorities included addressing the COVID-19 pandemic (both medically and economically), setting sweeping goals to address climate change, reforming immigration, and reversing corporate tax cuts.

Biden's tenure was filled with failures for the American people. Inflation rose to a level not seen since Jimmy Carter, 9% in one year. The inflation was due in part to his new rules for drilling for oil, making it more difficult and resulting in a 50% increase in fuel cost.

He set stringent rules in handling the pandemic that created hardships — divorces, suicides, lost businesses, even closed churches and perhaps most of all, robbed some children of almost 2 years of education.

He relaxed the rules that Trump used in bringing the border under control resulting in record number of illegals arriving. That added to our crime, smuggling of drugs especially fentanyl. Drugs caused the death of over 100,000 Americans per year. Crime multiplied as the Mexican cartels robbed, looted, raped and even murdered desperate immigrants. The cartel gangs and other gangs such as Venezuelan gangs came across the border and established themselves in America.

Biden threw away the plan that Trump had for evacuating Afghan resulting in the Taliban controlling the process. The biggest mistake was closing the military base that was the protection for evacuation and if kept, provided a convenient military presence in that part of the world. Biden basically threw away our advantage, our control of the evacuation and even 80 billion of high-tech military equipment now scattered among our enemies including Iran. That caused the death of 13 servicemen, many friends of America and chaos. The Afghan debacle may have been the worse ever by an American president. It showed ignorance of our military advantage and ignorance of who the Taliban was. Only a neophyte would perform such an un-American act.

Finally, he continued spending beyond the income that America had amassing nearly $10 trillion in additional debt. He continued throwing money at the pandemic and instead of monitoring the spending, letting crooks, mostly outside our country fraudulently take some unknown figure that some have approximated at $400 billion.

Much of his debt spending was spent on special interest friends of the Democrats such as education, environmental subsidies and the like. He even tried to pay student loans that totaled $1.6 trillion.

When election time rolled around again, Biden intended to run but in his first debate, it was obvious that he had severe senility hidden by the Democratic Party. We also learned that he spent 40% of his time on vacation so his leadership as president was almost missing. Apparently, the White House was run by some unknown group of people, not elected. I wonder if George Soros is on the board. When the general public saw the debate and realized his condition, the polls went down quickly and set him up to lose by a great number of votes. The Democrats then essentially made him give up his intent to run again although it was a considerable struggle. He was determined to hold on to the White House as long as he could. Still, he continues to carry the nuclear button for another 5-6 months until the next president has been inaugurated. It is telling that with this obvious handicap, almost all of the traditional democrats still were planning to vote for him. Loyalty before country?

Chapter 21
Final Word

As we reviewed the Democratic party, we learn that Democrats too often focus on special interest groups rather than America. For example, the effort to pay student loans by Joe Biden had nothing to do with the success of America and clearly appears to be an effort to use taxpayer money to buy votes. Paying student loans would open up a massive controversy and be an add of major proportions to a socialistic approach to government.

America's future depends upon action to stop the increase in debt and reduce what is already a dangerous amount, having grown from 10 trillion to 36 trillion in only 16 years. Today there is no plan in place to even reduce the rate of debt growth.

America's future depends to a large degree on the reduction of the illegal immigration of 15 to 20 million people including terrorists, criminals, people with no work skills and dependents in the last 4 years. The chaos caused by an immigration so high that border patrols cannot keep up with the quantity of illegals make it much easier to smuggle drugs at the same time. This immigration breaks a law every time an illegal is assimilated into our country. When enough people to populate New York City are allowed into the country in one presidential term imagine, in 10 terms we might double our population. One can only suspect that the purpose is to gain a large majority of the votes somewhere down the future. Maybe even to increase the fraudulent votes.

Our loss of jobs and manufacturing companies to China and other countries robs us of money. Our trade imbalance with China along with our technology as a gift has elevated them to the number 2 country in the world. They have used that position to seek the total takeover of Southeast Asia which they are signaling with some very aggressive moves. Tariffs are necessary and the extra product costs that that might cause is worth the money to keep jobs, keep the manufacturing of critical items such as computer chips and military weapons and keep America as a world leader. One can not expect something for nothing. Are we concerned about our pocket books or America.

Another frightening characteristic of recent democratic presidents is the timidity of the Democrats. They often start wars but don't finish them and communicate weakness which encourages our enemies and terrorists to be aggressive, not only enslaving and killing many people but endangering Americans at home and overseas.

America's voters have reached the point that Socrates predicted for a democracy. Once voters understand that they can receive more and more from the government by their vote, democracy will die. Buying votes is purely a socialistic action. Certainly, it seems everyone has their hand out and the Democrats answer is to tax the rich more when they already pay 90% of the taxes. There comes a time when enough is enough. You can only bend a branch a certain amount and then it will break. We are near the breaking point and the effort to buy votes and the desire by voters for a free lunch has to stop or we will turn into an Argentina, a bankrupt nation with no impact in the world.

www.ingramcontent.com/pod-product-compliance
Lightning Source LLC
Chambersburg PA
CBHW070644030426
42337CB00020B/4163